Awaken from Suffering: A Hero's Journey

Norman Brown

SILENCE

This book is dedicated to Luma.

Introduction

Awaken from Suffering: A Heros Journey

Between the banks of pleasure and pain, the river of life flows, and you are but a reed in that river.—Nisargadata Maharaj

This book represents the culmination of my 66-year spiritual journey, shaped by countless experiences, teachings, and personal revelations. Its content was born from the talks I gave at my retreat center on the island of Koh Phangan, Thailand, where, from 2000 to 2012, over 6,000 individuals came into our kitchen building, seeking personal growth.

The retreat center emerged during a period when I felt stalled on my spiritual path. Despite years of dedicated practice and study, I found myself without a path—teachers no longer held my interest, every book I read seemed to echo the same messages, and I felt as though I had reached the end of my spiritual road. One day, my wife turned to me and asked, "What's our next step?" I had no answer. That uncertainty hung over us for several years.

Then, everything changed during a near-death experience. I found myself lying nude on the bathroom floor of an Indian hotel in Bangalore, after four days of intense purging from a medication. In that harrowing moment, a message rang out: *"I want you to give all you have gained to others."* When I got up off that floor a few hours later, I knew my life had taken on a new purpose—one of service.

This revelation marked the beginning of a new chapter in my life, but the journey that led me to this book began much earlier. From the age of eight, I felt as if I were searching for something, though I couldn't articulate what it was. Nineteen years later, I discovered it in meditation. Meditation became the key that opened a door I never looked back on. Since then, each major breakthrough has felt like a new lifetime, with dramatic changes along the way.

While much of what I have learned has been through personal exploration, I have also received invaluable guidance at crucial times from spiritual teachers, whether in person, through books, or via videos. These experiences have been profound enough to fill an entire series of books.

Purpose: This book is designed to guide you on a hero's journey of self-discovery, transformation, and healing of past wounds that hold you back in life. Combining spirituality and psychology offers a holistic approach to personal growth, helping you navigate your emotional landscape and uncover your true potential.

Audience: During the twelve transformative years at my retreat center in Thailand, I had the privilege of meeting people from all walks of life—clergy, CEOs, artists, students, construction workers, husbands, and wives. This diversity attested to the universal need for personal growth. This book is for anyone feeling stuck, seeking profound change and emotional healing. It will especially benefit those who have found traditional self-help methods lacking and those interested in spirituality, mindfulness, and emotional well-being.

Many who came to our retreat center would say, "I've tried everything and reached the end of my rope. My life needed change, but nothing I've done has worked." I am not a magical wizard, but I have learned to distill spiritual concepts, personal experiences, and what I call innate wisdom into simple, accessible terms.

While the principles shared here may not be entirely new, the power lies in how they are presented. This book isn't about entertainment or intellectual novelty; it's about offering you compassion, understanding, and a genuine connection to the self. If you engage with these words, they can guide you back home to yourself. Within these pages—and the accompanying workbook—you'll find keys to change and hidden gems for personal growth.

Overview: In this book, I share the lessons and techniques that have helped countless people create meaningful life changes. Each chapter covers a specific aspect of emotional and spiritual growth:

- **Chapter One:** How to Create Life Changes–Techniques for self-observation and pattern interruption.

- **Chapter Two:** Transition of Emotions–Understanding and managing emotional cycles.

- **Chapter Three:** Social Conditioning–Identifying and challenging societal and familial conditioning.

- **Chapter Four:** The Dual Nature of Self–Balancing the light and dark aspects of our personalities.

- **Chapter Five:** Boundaries–Establishing and maintaining healthy boundaries.

- **Chapter Six:** Emotional Healing–Steps to recognize and heal emotional wounds.

- **Chapter Seven:** Accepting What Is–The power of acceptance and techniques to practice it.

Promise: For those of you who might be thinking, "I already know this stuff," I encourage you to keep this book on hand for those challenging days when nothing seems to be working. With a success rate of over 95% among individuals motivated to make significant life changes, the knowledge in this book is a trustworthy guide on your journey. By the end, you will have a deeper understanding of yourself, improved emotional resilience, and practical tools to create meaningful life changes. This journey is't just about learning new concepts—it's about transforming your life and finding your way home to yourself.

A Story about Having Patience with Your Process

A young man once came to me and shared his story. He spoke of childhood abuse and how he'd been lost in alcohol from an early age. "Is there anything you can do to help me?" he asked. He was broke, with only a return ticket back to England.

I offered him a job in exchange for the one-month course I was providing. He worked for the time agreed upon, and he became like a son to me during this time. I gave him the love and respect that he so desperately needed. It wasn't my plan or my intention. It just happened.

Then came the time for his course. Three weeks in, he ran away. We searched for him but couldn't find him. Two weeks later, we saw him by chance. He was drunk, shirtless, his jeans covered in gravel dust, and road rash all over his body.

In his stupor, he recognized us. We put him into the back of my pickup and two girls with me sat in the back of the truck and held him in their arms as we drove back to the retreat center. When we arrived, he jumped out of the truck, recognizing where he was. He pulled away from the girls, who were trying to lead him to one of the rooms to sleep.

He yelled, "I don't deserve this!" Tears streamed down his face—something he had never allowed himself to do. From a young age, he had vowed that nothing would touch him. He broke free from the girls who tried to guide him and ran down the hill. I shouted after him, "You deserve love! We love you!" We never heard from him again.

Everyone wrote him off as someone who would never change. Two years later, I heard from one of the girls there that night. She said he had met him by accident, and he had stopped drinking and was hard at work.

Five years after that, he sent me a card. Inside was a photo of a baby in his arms. The front read, "Thank you!" Inside, one line: *"This could never have happened without meeting you.'*

This is my promise to you. Though I am only here in spirit, together we can laugh, cry, and have profound experiences. You are not on this path alone. Think of me as the guy sitting on a fence post at a crossroads, taking a rest. You just asked me which direction home is, and I pointed to the road I took—the one less traveled. Good luck on your journey home. To you!

Patience, my ass! I'm going to kill something!

Chapter One
How to Create Life Changes

Prelude: A few pointers to start

My journey to self-discovery has been one of trial and error. I was my own guinea pig, experimenting along the way, trusting my inner guide to lead me toward self-realization.

The Vedas, ancient texts about life, speak of the "Sat Guru," or "Inner Teacher," that lies within each of us. If we trust this inner guide, it will lead us to the people, places, and situations we need to reach higher stages of self-awareness. Sometimes, this Sat Guru manifests as an external teacher. Throughout my journey, I have encountered many of these guides—from unknown Sadhus and spiritual teachers to Hindu saints and renowned authors on relationships.

This book is intended as a handshake, if you will, between spirituality and psychology. It is the path that I walked to get here. Despite devoting my entire adult life to the study of spirituality, I have no degree in psychology or spirituality. I used to tell my clients, "All this spiritual knowledge that I have and $5.00 will get you a cup of coffee."

This knowledge won't directly pay your bills or make you wealthy, but it can make you happy, content, and at peace. I'm sharing my journey as a series of lessons and a workbook for you to follow. It took me years of experience and teaching to arrive at Chapter One. This book aims to save you the trouble of sitting cross-legged on a temple floor for hours, enduring the heat and noise of India, or joining a spiritual organization that may not serve you in the end.

Most importantly, this book will help shorten your path to self-discovery and healing. By doing so, you'll have the potential for happiness and peace at an earlier age than I did. Who knows what your potential is? The earlier you can see and live it, the more profound your life can be.

When people thank me for helping them, I always say, *"I'm not here just for you. This is for everyone around you, for those you 'll meet, and for future generations."* When you change a single behavior for the better, it affects not just you but all those who follow. The old inheritance stops with you.

Self-awareness and the power of observation are essential to personal growth and spiritual enlightenment. So, let's begin.

Final thought: Don't get me wrong, I would do it all over again in a heartbeat and not change anything.

The Power of Observation

Observation is a fundamental technique for creating life changes. It starts with simply noticing your thoughts and behaviors without judgment. This awareness is often the first step toward meaningful transformation.

In my journey, I began by observing some of my negative behaviors without judgment. To my surprise, many of them simply faded away. Of course, some challenges required more effort—research, intentional action, and sometimes even therapy to overcome.

The difference between observation and judgment is crucial. When you observe, you simply notice what's happening without adding critique. Judgment, however, involves labeling behaviors as good or bad, often leading to guilt or defensiveness.

Non-judgmental observation allows you to see your actions with clarity, unclouded by self-criticism. With this clear view, you can understand the root causes of your actions and create a compassionate space where real change can occur. When you observe without judgment, you're more likely to accept what you see and take constructive steps toward change, rather than getting stuck in negative self-talk.

Think of self-awareness and observation as shining a light in a dark room. They illuminate the hidden corners of our behavior, enabling us to see clearly and make conscious choices. This practice is the foundation upon which the next key concept— pattern interruption—can be built.

Pattern Interruption

Pattern interruption is a technique to break automatic behaviors and make room for positive change. By identifying and interrupting negative patterns, you create the opportunity for transformation.

Now, simply choosing to interrupt a pattern doesn't always work. At least, it never did for me. Maybe it worked temporarily, but I often found myself falling right back into the old habit.

Think of a train running along a set track; unless you change its direction, it will continue indefinitely. Our behaviors are much the same. Pattern interruption involves consciously stepping off those tracks to choose a new path.

Challenges You Might Face

Breaking these patterns isn't easy. You might encounter roadblocks —overwhelming emotions, deeply ingrained habits, or feelings of discouragement. Here are some common challenges and ways to navigate them:

1. **Overpowering Emotions:** If observing a pattern stirs intense emotions, take a pause. This isn't a failure; it's part of the process. Sometimes, you'll uncover something deeply buried—a nugget of gold that looks like coal. In such cases, step back and give yourself time to process. You can return to observation later or seek support from a therapist or a trusted guide.

2. **Difficulty in Interrupting the Pattern:** Despite your best efforts, the pattern might persist. Remember, this is normal, especially for long-standing behaviors. Start with smaller changes to build confidence. Be patient; lasting change takes time.

Actionable Steps to Identify and Interrupt Behavior Patterns:

1. Set an Intention to Observe:

- Begin with a clear intention to observe your behavior patterns.
- **Example**: Decide to become more aware of a specific pattern, such as reacting with anger or feeling anxious in certain situations.

2. Commit to Being Present:

- Practice mindfulness to stay present when the behavior pattern occurs.
- **Example**: Use meditation or deep breathing techniques to center yourself and maintain awareness during triggering situations.

3. Observe Without Getting Caught Up:

- When the pattern arises, observe your emotional response without getting caught up in it.
- **Example**: Notice your feelings of anger, sadness, or anxiety, but refrain from acting on them or letting them dictate your behavior.

4. Allow Emotions to Be Present:

- Let your emotions exist without trying to change or suppress them.
- **Example**: Acknowledge your feelings, letting them pass through you without attaching to them or letting them control your actions.

5. Refrain from Self-Victimization and Blame:

- Avoid feeling sorry for yourself or blaming others for your emotional responses.
- **Example**: Acknowledge your feelings without assigning blame to yourself or others, focusing instead on understanding and accepting the experience.

6. Be Patient and Curious:

- Maintain a state of non-judgmental observation and be patient as you learn about the pattern.
- **Example**: Like a buzzard watching over a herd of cattle, be intensely curious and patient, allowing the pattern to repeat itself until you understand it fully.

7. Recognize the Moment for Change:

- Wait for the moment when you know you can change the direction of what is happening.

- **Example**: This moment of realization may come after many observations. When it does, any action to interrupt the pattern, such as jumping up and down, can create change.

8. Implement New Actions:

- Once you recognize the pattern and the moment for change, take a new action to interrupt the pattern.

- **Example**: Choose any action that breaks the pattern's groove and creates a new response. This pulls you out of the pattern and gives you a choice.

9. Reflect on Your Observations:

- After the situation has passed, reflect on what you observed and how you managed to stay present.

- **Example**: Consider what worked well and what could be improved for next time, reinforcing your commitment to positive change.

10. Stay Committed to Learning:

- Maintain a strong determination to learn and understand all you can about your behavior patterns.

- **Example**: Continuously seek knowledge, whether through personal reflection, reading, or discussing with others, to deepen your understanding and improve your responses.

11. Embrace Willingness, Commitment, and Determination:

- Approach each step with willingness, commitment, and determination.

- **Example**: Be willing to observe, commit to staying present, and be determined to understand and change your behavior patterns.

By focusing on observation and being present, you can gain greater control over your behavior patterns and create lasting positive change in your life. The ingrained pattern has both physiological and psychological roots. When you do things differently, you break free from the pattern and open up new choices—choices you didn't realize were there before.

Using this technique gave me the space to be more consciously aware. I began to set new patterns and implement actions that led to positive outcomes. Gradually, these new patterns replaced the old ones and, with time and patience, they became almost automatic. This was one of the first techniques I learned, and I still use it today. It's a long process, requiring a deep breath of patience, but it works.

Pattern Interruption in Action: A Woman and Her Coworker

A woman I worked with shared her story about a man at her office. Every day, he walked past her desk, which was near the entrance. She disliked him so much that she dreaded his arrival. To avoid any interaction, she would look away whenever he passed. The distress was so intense that she even asked her boss to move her to another part of the office.

I suggested that she try my technique: stay neutral and observe the situation without judgment. After the first week, she reported experiencing anxiety and fear. She still couldn't look him in the face, but she managed to observe herself and watch him as he approached.

In the second week, she finally mustered the courage to look at him. She felt a wave of terror as he walked by, but it subsided after he passed. On the third day, something shifted. When he came into view, she didn't just see him—she saw her uncle. His hair, forehead, and eyebrows mirrored those of her childhood tormentor.

Over the next few days, she continued looking at him as he passed. Each time, the initial terror gave way to curiosity. She started noticing the details: the unease in his step, the nervous glance he cast her way. Slowly, her fear began to fade.

Then came a breakthrough. Taking a deep breath, she did something out of character: she looked him in the eyes, smiled, and said, "Good morning." To her surprise, he softened and warmly returned the greeting. In that instant, the fear that had gripped her for weeks began to dissipate.

Encouraged by this connection, she made an effort to be friendly. Gradually, they started chatting each morning. To her surprise, he admitted that he, too, had felt apprehensive passing her desk, though he couldn't explain why.

Feeling empowered by this newfound connection and the dissolution of her fear, she shared her progress with me. We talked about exploring these feelings more deeply, and I suggested she seek support from a therapist. Through therapy, she uncovered a long-buried memory: her uncle had passed away when she was a little girl. The grief had been too overwhelming for her young mind to process. At first, she feared that something terrible might have happened between her and her uncle. The emotions had been buried and had unknowingly affected her interactions with men who resembled him.

With the therapist's help, she confronted and healed this wound. She learned from her parents that her uncle, who had no children of his own, had loved her dearly. The healing wasn't easy, but it allowed her to move forward without the shadow of unexplained fear. Her journey transformed not only her relationship with the man at work but also brought peace to a part of her past that had haunted her for years.

The Curiosity Technique

The curiosity technique harnesses the mind's natural problem-solving abilities to uncover the root causes of our reactions and behaviors. This approach promotes self-awareness and transformation by maintaining a neutral and curious mindset.

The mind is your servant, and it is in constant service to you. You must guide it to serve you in the most beneficial ways, much like ChatGPT. When you pose a question, it retrieves information to help you. Often, however, we aren't aware of this process, so the mind attempts to provide more of whatever occupies our thoughts most.

Curiosity is a powerful tool for self-discovery and personal growth. By approaching your thoughts and reactions with curiosity, you shift from reactive to investigative. Curiosity allows you to uncover the root causes of your patterns and behaviors, leading to deeper understanding and transformation.

How to Apply It:

Here is my technique to find answers: Treat your mind as a problem solver—it's designed to help you find solutions, recall forgotten names, or locate misplaced keys. The key is to give your mind a task and then let go. Have you ever noticed that once you stop trying to remember a name, it suddenly comes to you? This happens because you allow your mind to work in the background, solving the problem without pressure.

Instead of reacting (when I have the headspace), I say to myself, "Isn't that interesting? I would like to know more about that." I get upset every time Joe walks into the room I'm in. I would like to know more about that." It tells your mind that you are curious and would like to learn about the situation, maintaining a neutral position.

As long as you are in a heightened emotional state, it's challenging to respond neutrally or gain insight. But as soon as you calm down, you can say, "Isn't it interesting that I react this way when this happens? I'd like to know more about that." Your mind will then begin to present you with memories and events related to your pattern, much like the woman in the previous story. Once she reached a more neutral space, her mind revealed what had been triggering her.

For me, it was like a backward march to the beginning of the pattern. I would see how the pattern affected my life and the people that I hurt or affected in some way or another. This technique is very slow, and in the beginning, you may have to repeat patterns over and over many times before you reach the beginning. But as you continue to use it, it will get faster. Your mind does learn, and it will get familiar with it.

It worked for me. It worked for others. I believe it can work for you too.

Conclusion

Understanding and applying the techniques of observation, pattern interruption, and curiosity can significantly transform your life. These methods are not quick fixes but are practices that, with patience and persistence, can lead to profound personal growth and lasting change.

Throughout this book, you will learn how observing yourself can increase awareness of your behaviors and your life in general. Simply reading this book might trigger automatic changes within you. If you encounter any frightening, confusing, or anxiety-inducing realizations, please seek professional help. This advice applies across all the chapters in this book.

As we move forward, we will explore ways to cultivate an increased ability to be more consciously aware of ourselves and our surroundings. Remember, the journey to self-awareness is ongoing. Be kind to yourself as you navigate this continuous process.

And know that I'm here with you in spirit, offering guidance and support as you take each step on this path. This journey is yours, but you don't have to walk it alone.

Glossary for Chapter 1: How to Create Life Changes

1. **Self-Discovery:** The process of gaining insight into one's own character, desires, and potential. It involves exploring one's thoughts, emotions, and experiences to better understand oneself.

2. **Sat Guru:** A term from the Vedas, referring to the "Inner Teacher" or the true guide within each individual that leads them towards self-realization and higher stages of consciousness.

3. **Awareness:** The state of being conscious of one's thoughts, feelings, and surroundings. Awareness is crucial for recognizing and understanding one's behaviors and patterns.

4. **Consciousness:** The quality or state of being aware. It is the foundation for self-awareness and personal growth.

5. **Personal Experience:** Learning and growth derived from one's own life events and reflections rather than external teachings or readings.

6. **Observation:** The practice of watching and examining one's thoughts, feelings, and behaviors without judgment. Observation is a key technique for creating meaningful change.

7. **Non-Judgmental Observation:** Observing one's thoughts and behaviors without criticism or approval, which helps in understanding and changing negative patterns.

8. **Pattern Interruption:** A technique used to break the cycle of automatic behaviors and responses by introducing new, conscious actions. This creates space for positive changes to emerge.

9. **Curiosity Technique:** Approaching one's reactions and behaviors with curiosity, asking questions to understand the underlying causes without judgment. This promotes deeper self-awareness and transformation.

10. **Self-Reflection:** The practice of examining and contemplating one's thoughts, emotions, and actions to gain insight and understanding.

11. **Self-Compassion:** Treating oneself with kindness and understanding during moments of failure or difficulty. Self-compassion is essential for emotional healing and personal growth.

12. **Emotional Triggers:** Specific situations, people, or events that provoke a strong emotional response. Recognizing and understanding triggers helps in managing emotions and reactions.

13. **Therapeutic Techniques:** Methods used in therapy to help individuals understand and change their behaviors and thought patterns. These can include mindfulness, cognitive-behavioral techniques, and self-compassion practices.

14. **Physiological Response:** The body's automatic reactions to stimuli, such as increased heart rate, sweating, or changes in breathing patterns. Understanding these responses helps in managing emotions.

15. **Psychological Response:** The mental and emotional reactions to stimuli, including thoughts, feelings, and behaviors. Awareness of these responses is crucial for personal growth.

16. **Acceptance:** Embracing one's thoughts, feelings, and experiences without trying to change or resist them. Acceptance leads to greater peace and understanding.

17. **Inner Guide:** The intuitive sense or internal voice that directs one towards personal growth and self-realization. Trusting this guide is essential for meaningful change.

18. **Spiritual Knowledge:** Insights and understandings derived from spiritual experiences, teachings, and inner wisdom rather than formal education.

References for Chapter One: How to Create Life Changes

1. Ludwig, V. U., Brewer, J. A., & Brown, K. W. (2020). Self-Regulation Without Force: Can Awareness Leverage Reward to Drive Behavior Change? Perspectives on Psychological Science. DOI: 10.1177/1745691620931460

2. University of Pennsylvania. (2021). Self-awareness can drive behavior change, reprogram the brain's reward system. Retrieved from Medical Xpress

3. Cooley, C. H. (1902). Human Nature and the Social Order. Explores the concept of the "looking glass self," which describes how an individual's self grows out of society's interpersonal interactions and the perceptions of others. New York: Scribner's. More Information

4. Schwartz, S. H., & Cieciuch, J. (2020). Values as Motives: Implications for Theory, Methods, and Practice. European Journal of Personality. More Information

5. Blume, T., & Ramble, C. (2021). The Self: A Transpersonal Neuroanthropological Account. Neuroanthropology, University of California Press.

6. Rogers, C., & Farson, R. E. (1957). Active Listening. Explains how active listening is a technique used in psychology that can enhance the understanding of human relations. Open Textbook Library

The purpose of human life is to become more and more of what we can possibly be. –Norman Brown

Chapter Two
Transition of Emotions

Emotions are a fundamental part of the human experience, influencing our actions and reactions in countless ways. Understanding how emotions transition and evolve is crucial for personal growth and emotional well-being. In this chapter, we will delve into the nature of emotions, their transitions, and how to navigate these changes effectively.

Being human means being emotional. Emotions come and go. They don't need a reason to exist. While the mind will try to justify or explain them, sometimes it's enough to recognize: "I'm feeling this because I am human." Without emotions, our world would be as dull as a black-and-white painting. They bring color to our lives.

Understanding Emotions

Emotions are complex responses to our environment, thoughts, and interactions. They are not static; they constantly shift and change, influenced by internal and external factors. Recognizing the transient nature of emotions is the first step toward managing them effectively. The movie *What the Bleep Do We Know* has an entire section on emotions and how they affect us. Dr. Candace Pert from the movie has a great book about peptides and human emotions.

The Two Components of Emotions

1. The Eternal Nature of Emotions

Emotions, by their very nature, can often feel eternal. When we are in the grip of a powerful emotion—whether it's sadness, anger, joy, or fear—it can seem as though this feeling has always been there and will never change. This sense of timelessness can make the emotion feel all-consuming, as if it defines our entire reality.

This perception of emotions as eternal can intensify the experience, making it more difficult to manage and move through. In those moments, it's almost impossible to remember that emotions are, in fact, temporary.

Understanding that this sense of eternality is just a part of the emotional experience can be incredibly freeing. It allows us to take a step back and recognize that while the emotion feels overwhelming right now, it won't last forever.

2. The Cycle of Emotions

Emotions often follow a cyclical pattern. A trigger causes an emotion to arise, leading to a physical response—like crying or feeling excited. It lingers for some time before subsiding, making way for another feeling. When we allow emotions to be without judgment, they come, are experienced, and then pass on to the next. This natural ebb and flow is present throughout our waking lives. Being aware of this cycle helps us better manage our reactions and navigate the transitions.

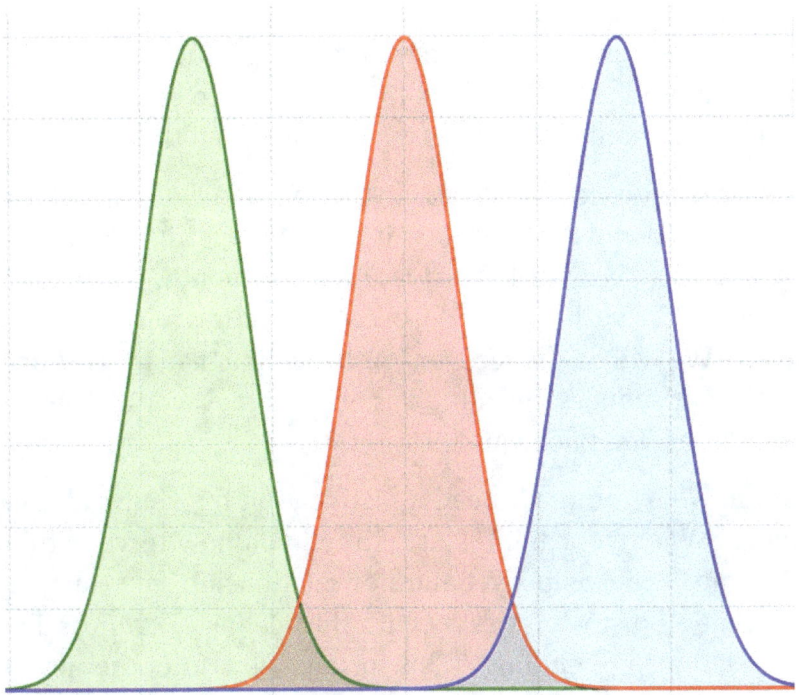

Emotions transiting from Envy to Anger to Sadness

Horizontal Represents Time and Vertical Represents Intensity

The Impact of the Mind and Its Thoughts on Emotions

When the mind tries to serve you, it often prolongs the peak of an emotion and revisits it over time. Take this example: your partner decides to end the relationship, and you feel the immediate sadness of the loss. In an attempt to help, your mind searches for similar situations where you've felt this way before.

Why does it do that? Because the nature of a feeling is eternal, and the mind will try to explain it through logic. It reminds you: "You were sad last week. You were sad last month. You were sad last year. You've been sad forever." Then, it projects into the future: "We will be sad forever." And just like that, in its effort to justify your sadness, the mind has made things worse. The truth is, emotions don't need justification.

Just knowing you don't need a justification for your sadness is enough. When your mind starts to tell you how terrible things are because you've lost yet another relationship, you can gently intervene: "I just want to stay with this feeling of sadness about the relationship ending." This brings you into the present moment, allowing you to experience the sadness without projecting future outcomes. By staying with the current feeling, you allow the emotion to move through you more quickly.

Understanding this cyclic pattern and the sense of eternality or eternal nature of emotions can help you anticipate and prepare for emotional changes. Once you know how emotions work, you can transit emotions easier and faster than ever. You don't stop them, and you don't push them away. Feel them. Just know that your mind will try to reinforce them in an attempt to serve you.

With your newfound knowledge, you can save yourself from long-lasting, deep feelings that are not necessary. It is not natural to suppress feelings or replace them with a possible outcome in the future. By practicing this technique, soon, you will have more control over your thoughts and feelings.

Personal Experience: A Journey Through Pain to Self-Love

Shortly after my wife left my life, I had a powerful and unexpected emotional experience while shopping at a Whole Foods store. As I turned down an aisle, a vivid memory of an argument we'd had over a supplement suddenly struck me. Beneath the anger from that memory, I discovered a deep, eternal love for her.

Overwhelmed by this realization, I began to cry uncontrollably in the store. It felt as though a dam had broken, unleashing a flood of emotions. Abandoning my cart, I rushed to my truck, tears streaming as I knew I needed to return home to process what was happening.

Once home, I collapsed onto the floor, curling up in agony. The pain I felt was unlike anything I had ever experienced. It was as though I was being torn apart by the loss, the sadness, and the memories of our life together.

Thoughts about previous relationships started to appear in my mind, and I asked, "Please! I want to stay with this loss." The other losses faded away, and my mind was flooded with memories of love, fun, and joy streamed through my mind.

I lay there in a ball, suffering the most incredible pain of loss and sorrow and sadness I had ever experienced in my life.

I was there for about an hour. The pain came in waves.

Then, it slowly subsided. At that moment, I felt as if a switch had been flipped. I felt an overwhelming wave of realization and clarity. The transition was instantaneous; I finally sat up and felt as though I was reborn. I had let go of something. I realized that in my desire to be loved, I had abandoned myself for the sake of being loved.

I stood up and gazed out the window at the trees. It felt as though nature itself acknowledged my pain. "We feel your pain and understand," seemed to be the message. As the wind blew through the trees, their branches swayed and intertwined, forming a heart shape. This sight felt like a personal affirmation.

This experience was a turning point in my life. It was as if I had tapped into a wellspring of self-love that I had never known before. The warmth that filled me was indescribable, and it brought with it a sense of peace and self-acceptance that I had never known before.

I was filled with self-acceptance and self-care. The words, "She is gone, but I am here for you always." I heard myself say. I had retrieved what I had just given away in self-abandonment.

Again, the crying, but this time, it was tears of joy and love for myself in a way I had not felt before.

Since that experience, I have never felt alone again. After my divorce, I spent seven years mostly reclusive and alone. I never felt lonely anytime during those seven years. I'm not saying that I was over the relationship at that point or that I didn't feel loss or sadness again.

Story review

I saw that my commitment to experiencing my feelings facilitated a breakthrough that changed how I saw and felt about myself.

If I had allowed myself to go into the memories of the past that my mind was starting to show me. I would have gone into a pity party and would not have had this personal transformation.

From a psychological perspective, this experience can be understood as a powerful example of how fully experiencing and processing emotions can lead to significant personal transformation. When we allow ourselves to feel our emotions without judgment, we create the space for healing and growth.

The mind, in its attempt to protect us, often tries to distract or rationalize our feelings, but when we stay present with our emotions, we can move through them and come out the other side with greater clarity and understanding.

This process of emotional catharsis is not just a release of pent-up feelings but a reorganization of our internal emotional landscape. By facing the pain head-on, I was able to reclaim a part of myself that I had lost in the relationship. I had thrown my self-love into a pit of self-abandonment for the sake of wanting to be loved.

This self-retrieval allowed me to move forward with a renewed sense of self-love and inner strength.

Story Takeaway

By allowing ourselves to fully experience and process our emotions without judgment, we create the space for healing and personal growth.

This experience serves as a reminder that while pain is inevitable, suffering is optional—how we engage with our emotions can determine whether we remain stuck or move forward in our journey.

Final Thoughts

Emotional transitions are a natural part of life. Understanding and accepting this allows you to navigate your emotions with greater ease and resilience.

Always think of your mind as your friend who has always served you to the best of its ability. However, it is now time to take control of your life and direct the mind to serve you in the most powerful ways possible.

One effective way to achieve this is to let your mind step aside when you are feeling something, and you will call you if you need help.

Embrace the journey of emotional self-discovery and use the techniques provided in this chapter to support your emotional well-being.

Glossary for Chapter 2: Transition of Emotions

1. **Emotional Transition:** The process by which emotions change or evolve over time, crucial for emotional well-being and personal growth.

2. **Emotions:** Complex psychological states that involve physiological arousal, expressive behaviors, and conscious experience, influencing our thoughts, behaviors, and interactions.

3. **Eternality of Emotions:** The perception that emotions are all-pervasive and unchanging, making them feel more intense and long-lasting than they actually are.

4. **Cyclic Nature of Emotions:** The pattern of emotions rising, peaking, and then subsiding. Recognizing this cycle helps in managing emotional responses.

5. **Mind-Emotion Interaction:** The relationship between thoughts and emotions, where the mind often tries to justify or explain emotions through logical reasoning.

6. **Acceptance:** The process of acknowledging and embracing emotions without judgment, which helps in reducing the intensity and duration of negative emotions.

7. **Self-Reflection:** The practice of examining one's own thoughts, feelings, and behaviors to gain insight and understanding, crucial for emotional healing.

8. **Forgiveness:** The act of letting go of resentment and anger towards oneself or others, important for emotional healing and personal growth.

9. **Emotional Triggers:** Specific events, people, or situations that provoke a strong emotional response. Identifying and understanding triggers is key to managing emotions.

10. **Emotional Baggage:** Unresolved emotional issues from the past that affect current behavior and relationships. Addressing emotional baggage is essential for healthy emotional transitions.

11. **Core Beliefs:** Deep-seated beliefs that influence how we perceive and respond to situations, often stemming from early experiences and shaping our emotional responses.

12. **Self-Compassion:** Treating oneself with kindness and understanding during times of emotional distress, promoting healing and resilience.

13. **Mindfulness:** The practice of being present and fully engaged with the current moment, helping in observing emotions without judgment.

14. **Emotional Awareness:** The ability to recognize and understand one's own emotions, the first step towards managing them effectively.

15. **Emotional Healing:** The process of acknowledging, understanding, and resolving emotional wounds, involving self-reflection, acceptance, and forgiveness.

16. **Letting Go:** Releasing the need to control or change emotions, allowing them to flow naturally, a key component of emotional healing.

17. **Therapeutic Techniques:** Methods used in therapy to help individuals manage and resolve emotional issues, including mindfulness, cognitive reframing, and self-compassion exercises.

18. **Self-Destructive Behaviors:** Actions that harm oneself emotionally or physically, often stemming from unresolved emotional issues and needing to be addressed for emotional healing.

References for Chapter Two: Transition of Emotions

- Emotions are inherently transient, fluctuating due to various internal and external stimuli. According to research, emotions such as happiness, sadness, and anger are not permanent states but are influenced by our interactions and environments (The Eden Magazine).

- The concept of emotional cycles, where emotions arise, peak, and then transition to other states, is well-documented. Recognizing this pattern can help in managing emotional responses more effectively (Frontiers in Psychology).

- The brain's neural circuits play a crucial role in how we experience and regulate emotions. Studies have shown that different emotions involve overlapping neural networks, which contribute to the fluid nature of our emotional experiences (Neurobiology of Emotion).

- Emotions can be intensified by the mind's attempt to justify and explain them, often leading to prolonged emotional states. Understanding this cognitive process can help in mitigating its impact (Behavioral and Neurobiological Convergence).

- Mindfulness practices have been shown to help in managing emotions by promoting awareness and acceptance of the present moment. This approach reduces the mind's tendency to dwell on negative emotions and enhances emotional regulation (ScienceDirect).

- Techniques such as journaling, self-compassion exercises, and mindfulness meditation are supported by research as effective methods for processing and managing emotions (The Eden Magazine).

Studies on Emotional Transitions:

- "The Emotional Transition to Stable Life Change" (Psychology Today): Discusses how mindfulness and acceptance can help manage emotional transitions, focusing on the stages of loss, chaos, and new beginnings.

Books on Emotional Regulation:

- "Emotional Worlds: Beyond an Anthropology of Emotion" (Cambridge University Press): Explores the anthropology of emotions, emphasizing how different cultures understand and manage emotions, which can provide additional insights into emotional transitions.

- Psychological Anthropology: Exploring the Human Mind Across Cultures": Covers various psychological topics, including emotion, and provides a cross-cultural perspective on emotional experiences and transitions.

Videos on Emotional Healing and Mindfulness:

- TEDx Talks on Emotional Resilience and Healing: These talks often include practical advice and scientific insights into managing emotions and building resilience.

- Psych2Go on Understanding and Managing Emotions: Offers accessible explanations and tips for emotional regulation and self-awareness.

This is me teaching a class on how to remove manure (Conditioning) from your life.

Chapter Three
Social Conditioning

Introduction

Imagine growing up in a household where your mother dressed you each morning and getting dirty could result in dire consequences. Add to that, certain rooms were off-limits, and stepping inside them meant a severe spanking. The house was always spotlessly clean. Now, consider how that might shape your feelings towards controlling your environment as an adult.

By the way, this poor child ran away from home at 14. Her mother saw her once after that. Her hair was matted and tangled with lice, and she had hardly taken baths or showers.

In this chapter, we'll explore the concept of social conditioning—the process by which we learn and adopt societal norms, values, and behaviors—impacts our actions and self-perception. This process starts from a very young age and continues throughout our lives, influencing our actions and thoughts often without us even realizing it. Our ability to adapt to our environment has been crucial for survival, but it also means that conditioning plays a significant role in shaping who we become.

Understanding Social Conditioning

Social conditioning begins the moment you are born. From family dynamics to cultural expectations, every aspect of your environment molds your understanding of what is acceptable and desirable. These influences form the foundation of your beliefs, values, and behaviors.

Personal Reflection:

In my family, discipline was nonexistent. As a result, I didn't learn it as a child. No one checked if I was doing my homework, so I didn't bother. I cruised through school, doing only the minimum to pass. The only subject I excelled at was math because I enjoyed it. Five minutes before class, I would do the homework at my desk, trying to get as far as possible before class started. Consequently, I got the highest grades on my tests and better than average on my homework, even though I didn't finish it.

When I graduated, my grades weren't enough to get into university, and we couldn't afford it anyway. I ended up working for Hallmark Greeting Cards, supplying workers on the assembly line. There was no chance for advancement except maybe becoming a supervisor after many years. Now there is nothing wrong with a job like that. But, for me, it seemed incredibly limiting for advancement and for money. This experience taught me a valuable lesson: if you want to go somewhere in life, you have to make a change.

Reflective Questions:

- Reflect on your childhood. What were some of the unspoken rules in your household? How do you see those rules playing out in your life today?
- What was the environment in your home like when you were a child?
- How did you see the interactions between your family members?
- How did you see each of their relationship with you?

The Role of Family, Society, and Religion

Our families, societies, and religions play significant roles in shaping our identities. Family teaches us our first lessons about the world and our place in it. Society provides us with broader norms and expectations, while religion often offers a moral framework for understanding right and wrong. These forces create a powerful influence that shapes our worldview and behaviors.

Family

The Preverbal Stage

From birth, infants are profoundly influenced by their environment. They are in a constant state of observation, gathering data to understand their surroundings. Despite being unable to articulate their experiences, babies are deeply affected by the emotional atmosphere around them. For instance, a baby growing up in a household with frequent arguments absorbs that tension, making it a familiar feeling. As adults, these individuals might find themselves in similar relationships, unconsciously recreating the environment they were conditioned to during this preverbal stage.

Conversely, a baby raised in a calm, nurturing environment may grow up feeling secure and trusting. These early preverbal experiences lay the foundation for future emotional, psychological, and social development, significantly influencing how we respond to stress, form relationships, and perceive the world. This highlights the crucial role parents, caregivers, and educators play in shaping a child's early years.

One intriguing aspect of the preverbal stage is that once we develop language, we lose direct access to these early life experiences. Yet, this period continues to shape our decisions throughout life. For example, if you find yourself feeling an inexplicable attraction to someone, it might be your preverbal stage trying to recreate a familiar environment.

In chapter four, we will discuss how we create our reality. This will help you understand what I will say next and free you from the effects of the preverbal stage.

The next time you look at someone and feel incredibly attracted to them and don't understand why, it may not be anything other than the preverbal stage trying to reestablish its environment. The influence of these early experiences on our decision-making processes is a testament to the enduring impact of the preverbal stage.

Personal Story:

My interest in social influences during the preverbal period began with an incident involving my second daughter when she was a baby. We were all getting ready to go somewhere, and my wife had just finished dressing our new baby, who was only a few months old, and she put her in the car seat on the kitchen counter.

We gathered around her because she was in such a joyful mood. We fussed over her, laughing and cooing at how sweet she was. It was a lovely, heartwarming moment. But then, suddenly, her laughter stopped. She looked at each of us, and her face scrunched up in sheer terror. In an instant, she broke into a frantic cry. We were stunned. My wife quickly picked her up, trying to comfort and reassure her.

This moment left me both shocked and curious about how our actions and environment affect children, even at such a young age.

Later in life, I developed some techniques that could help with the preverbal stage to help heal.

Resources:

In the reference section for this chapter, you'll find resources specifically related to the preverbal stage. If you notice behaviors in yourself that seem to lack a clear source, these references may offer programs that can help. I also provide programs designed to support you in working on childhood issues independently or with a therapist as needed.

Toddler to Puberty

During early childhood, you see the world revolving around you, a kind of universality or oneness. Another way to say this is that you see yourself as the center of everything. This self-centered worldview can extend into the teenage years, leading to thoughts like, "If I weren't here, Mom and Dad wouldn't be fighting."

Imagine a small child playing under the kitchen table while their mom prepares breakfast. In a rush, Mom puts bread in the toaster, but it doesn't work. Frustrated, she fiddles with it briefly before tossing it in the trash, saying to her husband, "I'll pick up a new one after work."

To the child, who doesn't yet differentiate between people and inanimate objects, this situation registers as a simple rule: when things are broken, they are discarded. This belief is reinforced by the immediate action of throwing away the toaster.

Then, one day, Dad comes home with a new car and surprises everyone. He explains that the old car broke down on the way home, so he towed it to the dealer and got a new one. The child's understanding deepens: if something breaks, it gets replaced.

Later, Mom returns from the hospital with a new baby. To the child, this situation might suggest that they are broken and have been replaced. All the attention previously focused on the first child is now diverted to the new baby. The child perceives this as reinforcement of the idea that being replaced is the outcome of being broken.

The child may not consciously think these things, but these experiences have a subconscious effect. They shape the child's understanding of themselves and their place in the family, leading them to interpret the situation as punishment or inadequacy.

These early beliefs can have a lasting influence, affecting how we perceive ourselves and our relationships throughout life.

Personal Experience

When my oldest daughter was around two, I was taking an introductory psychology course. One day, while my wife was at work, I put my daughter to bed and went back to the living room to study. Not long after, she began to cry. I went to her room, and she stopped. As soon as I left, she started crying again.

Having just learned that children around two to three years old start to understand that people still exist when they are not in the room, I decided to test the theory. I went to her room and asked what she needed, but she didn't know. So, I stepped out and stood just out of sight in the hallway. Sure enough, she started crying again.

Then, I decided we would play a game. I would step into the doorway so she could see me while I talked to her. I explained to her exactly what we were doing. I talked nonstop into the doorway and then back out of site. Continuing to talk. As I spoke to her, I reassured her that just because she didn't see me, it doesn't mean I am gone.

We practiced this a bit, and she seemed to grasp the idea. To test it further, I extended the experiment by going all the way to the living room, talking the entire time. I called out, asking if she could hear me from there. When she confirmed that she could, I returned to her room. I then asked if she would feel comfortable with me staying in the living room and reminded her that if she needed me, all she had to do was call out. She agreed, saying it seemed like a fair solution.

I returned to the living room and started to study. About two minutes later, I heard her call out to me. I responded and she said, I think I can go to sleep now.

Was this a real experiment, or did she want my attention until she was tired enough to go to sleep? All I can say is that we never had much of a problem with her going to bed after that. A bit further reflection: it is sad to say that was the end of her constantly needing to sleep with us.

A Brief Digression:

About a week after she began sleeping in her own bed, my wife called out as we all settled in for the night: "Do you want to come sleep with us?"

"No, I want to sleep in my own little bed," our daughter answered. My wife and I exchanged looks—equal parts sadness and joy. Our little girl was taking her first steps toward independence. And we, for a change, would get a full night's sleep.

Reflection on Early Experiences

This experience with my daughter confirmed what I was learning in my psychology course and deepened my understanding of how children develop trust and security. It reminded me that these early interactions lay the foundation for navigating relationships and emotions throughout our lives. I can't help but think about how many of us were left to figure out on our own and how much of a difference it might have made to discover these things together in partnership with our parents.

School Age

From that point until adulthood, we are thrust into a world of societal conditioning. From here, it is peer conditioning, then societal conditioning, and the effects of religion on a culture's conditioning. You may not think you are affected by religion, but look at things like your relationship with the concept of good and evil, the movies you watch, and the books you read. It is in there, and it affects you.

You think you are your own agent, but you are not. You are the result of years of being told who, what, when, and where. And all during this time, being an adaptive creature to survive, you created survival techniques. It's completely understandable why teenagers rebel.

Unraveling social conditioning is a long, often lifelong process. But as you start to strip away these layers, you begin to discover your true self—something more beautiful than you ever imagined.

Self-Conditioning

Preface to Self-Conditioning

Trigger Warning: Some of what you are about to read may be triggering. It might stir up overwhelming memories you've suppressed or resurface unresolved pains. If at any point you feel uncomfortable, **STOP!** Take a break and see if the feelings subside. If they don't, consider seeking professional help and explaining what triggered you.

If the feelings subside and you choose not to seek help, skip the self-conditioning section and approach it when you are not doing it alone.

For those who read this warning and think, "What was the fuss about?"—just know, this warning wasn't meant for you.

Please bear with me in this next section because it is a little long, but you will be happy once we get through it. We are about to take an intense journey together.

Case Study:

A woman I worked with once shared that her mother struggled with alcoholism. After her father's death, which left only a small inheritance, her mother's drinking spiraled out of control. At just five years old, this girl became the adult of the house—cleaning, cooking, and caring for her mother. She missed out on her childhood entirely.

Imagine growing up under constant uncertainty, never knowing what will happen next. To her, her mother's behavior was normal. If something went wrong, it was her fault. Her mother's unpredictable behavior constantly made her feel inadequate and inept at the task of taking care of both of them. If her mother collapsed in a drunken state, she would wonder, *Is she dead? What will happen to me now?*

As an adult, she took everything seriously—even her fun. She became a force to be reckoned with in the business world, yet she harbored deep anger toward her mother. She was always in survival mode. Picture her trying to sell you a new car or some stock on the market. Can you guess my suggestion to her? Spend time with children. Continue doing so until you relearn how to play. Children are more than happy to teach you.

Of course, this was only one of many techniques she used to build a life worth living. In her case, play became the trigger that broke down her overly serious demeanor. She knew her situation backward and forward, but playing with children helped her connect with the magic of play on a feeling level—not just through logic or by powering through it, as she had done in her childhood.

The stories I share with you of people who have come to our courses to seek answers and find change are not people with mental illnesses. Something wasn't working in their lives, and they were seeking solutions. They are stories of people like you and me. They have endured hardships, sometimes forgetting them, or remembering without realizing the impact on their lives. As adults, the survival mechanisms they developed as children often become detrimental to their well-being.

Another Case Study: How Repetitive Actions Become Unconscious Behaviors

A man once told me about his childhood. When he was six or seven, his father was a mean drunk. With no mother and only a couple of siblings, he grew up without the nourishment of a loving touch. His father wanted nothing more than to keep him out of sight, punishing him with beatings whenever he disobeyed.

One day, he was doing something that his father didn't like, and the father yelled at him to come to him. The little boy ran up to his father, and his father yelled at him and grabbed him by the hair, picked him up in the air, shook him, and threw him aside like a piece of trash. Despite the pain that he experienced, he finally had some form of contact with his father other than beatings.

After that, he played a game. He would run up to his father, hoping to be grabbed by the hair and shaken. The boy even mimicked the action, pulling at his own hair to show what he wanted.

It wasn't until he was 28 that he remembered this behavior. Over time, he had grown to hate his father. When he was older, he beat his father in a rage before leaving home. By the time we met, he, too, was struggling with alcoholism, seeking answers and healing.

Coming to terms with the lack of love he had experienced as a child was a deeply healing experience for him. This is the man I mentioned at the beginning of the book—the one who sent me a photo five years later of his newborn baby. Before this, he had never considered having children, fearing he couldn't love them because his experience of love was so negative. He worried he might repeat the cycle of abuse. How does this happen?

Conditioned Survival Skills that We Create as Children

As children, we create survival skills. These are techniques that an **undeveloped** mind creates to survive whatever it determines to threaten our lives or safety and security. Here are just a few:

- A five-year-old girl pulled a chair up to the stove to cook.
- A six-year-old boy makes physical contact with his father by grabbing him by the hair, shaking him, and throwing him.

- A thirteen-year-old girl goes every day to a 40-something man so he can violently sexually abuse her because her mother constantly tells her that she is worthless.

- The five-year-old girl loses her childhood and becomes too serious as an adult and can't keep a relationship.

- The six-year-old boy has never experienced kindness because he drinks and fights as an adult and can't keep a job or a relationship.

- The thirteen-year-old girl seeks value through violent sexual abuse and, as an adult, continually has relationships with physically abusive men.

Yes, these are challenging stories to read about. It was just as difficult for these people to realize what they had created to survive. You can't blame a child for their decisions to help you survive. So, how can you fault yourself for what you created?

You did the best you could with what you had to work with. Forgiveness and understanding serve in the process of change. Forgive yourself. Forgive that child who did the best they could. Help them find peace as well as yourself.

The only reason that the child in you is still acting this out with you is because you are their only hope. If you turn away from them and do not answer this call that they are constantly showing you, then you are turning away from yourself, your happiness, and a child who knew no better.

What would you do if you walked into the house with the mother passed out on the couch and the five-year-old cooking at the stove?

Or, saw a drunk father pick up his child by the hair and shake him and throw him to the side like a piece of trash?

If you were walking down the street and saw this sweet thirteen-year-old girl, and you knew where she was going and what would happen?

They did those things for you as much as they did for themselves. They loved you so much and wanted you to live. Revisiting this brings tears to my eyes, not just because of the sadness of these people's events. But because of the redemption they found, the catharsis they went through in making peace with that child within when forgiveness happened, there was nothing to solve, nothing to do. Only love is left.

And a child is peacefully sleeping in your arms. As the emotional waves subside, and with a heart now open to change, let's focus on the practical steps that can guide us through this healing journey.

This process of emotional catharsis is not just about releasing pent-up feelings but about reorganizing our internal emotional landscape. By facing the pain head-on, we can reclaim parts of ourselves lost in the struggle and move forward with a renewed sense of self-love and inner strength.

You already know what happened to the boy with the cruel father.

The serious woman was depressed and about to lose her marriage. She is now content with herself and more relaxed in her life. And she no longer needs antidepressants. The second lady no longer attracts abusive men and continues to seek therapy from time to time to heal her relationship with her mother.

How did they do it? I teach a technique called "Inner Child." It allows you to interact with the child within who suffered the life-threatening event. Therapists use inner child work, and there is also audio that you can use.

I learned the technique that I use from a spiritual teacher nonverbally. It's not something that I would write here, and you follow it. I highly recommend that it be done with a professional. This is incredibly powerful work.

As we age, the survival techniques we develop in childhood often become unconscious behaviors that can hinder our happiness and personal growth. Both social and self-conditioning play a significant role in shaping who we are and where our lives take us. While not all conditioning is negative, if you feel your life isn't working for you, social and self-conditioning may be at least partly to blame. Fortunately, we don't have to remain stuck in these patterns. There are ways to break free. As we explore this book together, we will uncover hidden truths and healing methods. I'll be here to guide you on your journey toward self-discovery and healing, helping you awaken to your truest self.

The Concept of "Inheritance"

1. Defining Inheritance:

I refer to the set of beliefs, values, and behaviors we absorb in childhood as "The Inheritance." It is the psychological and emotional legacy passed down from generation to generation. While some aspects of our inheritance can be positive and supportive, others can be limiting and detrimental to our growth. We have choices. We don't have to accept this inheritance. We can leave it behind to rest in peace with our ancestors.

2. Distinguishing Inheritance from Genetic Traits:

There have been studies about DNA carrying diseases, features, and characteristics. But this is not the kind of inheritance that I'm talking about.

3. Mirroring and Behavioral Inheritance:

One form of inheritance is the idea that you behave just like your parent. You act like the particular parent because of what is called mirroring. A parent behaves in a particular way, good or bad. You see it, and to create familiarity, you imitate it. It can also be because of an unconscious desire to be accepted or loved by that parent.

4. Breaking the Cycle:

There is a saying, *"The apple doesn't fall far from the tree,"* suggesting that children will inevitably inherit their parents' traits and behaviors. While this may often seem true, it's not an absolute rule. Through conscious effort and healing, we have the power to break these inherited patterns and forge our own paths. You are not bound to repeat the mistakes of the past; instead, you can choose to cultivate a life that reflects your true self. Although this may be true, it is not always the case. You can heal, and these things don't have to happen.

5. Your Potential for Change:

You can leave these two inheritances behind and be whoever you want to be. All things are possible in this phenomenal universe. Remember earlier, I said you are not your own agent. You are a product of conditioning. That is the old you! You are already on a path of change. Take courage; we are on our way.

Are you ready? Let's challenge that shirt!

Challenging Social Conditioning

Awareness is the first step toward breaking free from social conditioning. By questioning the beliefs and behaviors you've adopted, you open yourself to new possibilities. This self-awareness allows you to identify which aspects of your conditioning no longer serve you and replace them with more authentic, empowering beliefs. This workbook will guide you deeper into this process.

Techniques to Challenge Social Conditioning: Actionable Steps

1. **Journaling:** Keep a journal to track your thoughts and behaviors. Reflect on situations where you felt compelled to act a certain way and question why. Writing down your experiences can help you see patterns and understand the influence of social conditioning.

2. **Mindful Observation:** Practice observing your thoughts and reactions without judgment. When you notice a conditioned response, take a moment to understand its origin. Ask yourself if this belief or behavior truly serves you.

3. **Seek Diverse Perspectives:** Expose yourself to different cultures, ideas, and viewpoints. Diverse perspectives can help you see beyond your conditioning and recognize alternative ways of thinking and being.

I did this myself. Traveling and living in different cultures. Meeting people I would never have met.

4. **Therapy and Counseling:** A professional can help you uncover deep-seated conditioning and provide tools to reframe and change these patterns. You can also take self-help courses.

Personal Experience with Social Conditioning

Growing up, I was taught to adhere to the norms and expectations of my family and society. However, as I embarked on my spiritual journey, I realized that many of these conditioned beliefs were not aligned with my true self. They did not serve me.

How did I know that they didn't serve me? Well, they made me unhappy or they negatively interfered with my life–it's simple. Through self-reflection and observation, I could identify and let go of these limiting beliefs, allowing me to live a more authentic and fulfilling life.

In my experience of grieving the loss of my wife, If I had allowed myself to go into the memories of the past that the mind was starting to show me, I would have gone into a pity party and would not have had this personal transformation.

In Closing

Other techniques in the book will help you untangle the conditioning we all receive. Many books on the effects of conditioning are available. If you find this subject fascinating or a possible solution, then try these books and videos.

Glossary for Chapter 3

1. Social Conditioning: The process by which individuals learn and adopt the norms, values, and behaviors of their society. This process influences actions, thoughts, and self-perception, often without conscious awareness.

2. Family Dynamics: The patterns of interaction and relationships within a family. Family dynamics play a crucial role in shaping an individual's beliefs, values, and behaviors.

3. Preverbal Stage: The developmental period in infancy before a child acquires language. Experiences during this stage can have a lasting impact on a person's emotional and psychological development.

4. Toddler to Puberty Stage: The developmental period from early childhood to the onset of puberty. During this time, children learn social norms and values through interactions with family, peers, and society.

5. Societal Conditioning: The influence of broader societal norms, values, and expectations on an individual's behavior and beliefs. This conditioning is reinforced through institutions such as schools, media, and community.

6. Peer Conditioning: The impact of peers and social groups on an individual's behavior and beliefs. Peer conditioning is especially significant during adolescence.

7. Religious Conditioning: The influence of religious beliefs and practices on an individual's values and behaviors. This conditioning can shape moral frameworks and cultural norms.

8. The Inheritance: A concept referring to the set of beliefs, values, and behaviors passed down from one generation to the next. This psychological and emotional legacy can impact an individual's life choices and self-perception.

9. Journaling: The practice of writing down thoughts, feelings, and experiences to gain insight and self-awareness. Journaling can help identify patterns of social conditioning.

10. Mindful Observation: The practice of observing one's thoughts and reactions without judgment. This technique helps in recognizing conditioned responses and understanding their origins.

11. Diverse Perspectives: Exposing oneself to different cultures, ideas, and viewpoints. This practice can broaden understanding and challenge conditioned beliefs.

12. Therapy and Counseling: Professional support to help individuals uncover and address deep-seated conditioning. Therapy can provide tools to reframe and change unproductive patterns.

13. Conditioned Responses: Automatic reactions learned through repeated exposure to certain stimuli or situations These responses are often unconscious and can shape behavior and interactions.

14. Cultural Norms: Shared expectations and rules that guide behavior within a society or group. Cultural norms are a significant aspect of social conditioning.

15. Self-Reflection: The process of introspectively examining one's thoughts, feelings, and behaviors. Self-reflection is essential for understanding the impact of social conditioning.

16. Behavioral Patterns: Recurring ways of acting that are influenced by past experiences and social conditioning. Identifying these patterns is crucial for personal growth and change.

17. Cognitive Reframing: A therapeutic technique that involves changing the way one thinks about a situation to alter emotional responses. This technique can help in addressing negative effects of social conditioning.

18. Emotional Awareness: The ability to recognize and understand one's own emotions. Emotional awareness is key to managing the impact of social conditioning.

19. Adaptive Behavior: Actions and responses that help individuals cope with their environment. Adaptive behavior can be positive or negative, depending on how it aligns with one's values and well-being.

20. Subconscious Beliefs: Deep-seated beliefs that operate below the level of conscious awareness. These beliefs often influence behavior and decision-making.

21. Emotional Regulation: The ability to manage and respond to emotional experiences in a healthy way. This involves being aware of and understanding one's emotions, as well as using strategies to regulate them.

22. Attachment Theory: A psychological model describing the dynamics of long-term and short-term interpersonal relationships. It is important in understanding how early experiences with caregivers influence one's emotional and social development.

23. Cognitive Dissonance: The mental discomfort experienced by a person who holds two or more contradictory beliefs, values, or ideas simultaneously. This concept can be relevant in understanding the conflict that arises from challenging social conditioning.

24. Neuroplasticity: The brain's ability to reorganize itself by forming new neural connections throughout life. This concept is crucial in understanding how individuals can change conditioned behaviors and thought patterns.

25. Implicit Bias: The attitudes or stereotypes that affect our understanding, actions, and decisions in an unconscious manner. Recognizing implicit bias can be a part of challenging social conditioning.

26. Intergenerational Trauma: Psychological effects that the experience of trauma experienced in one generation can have on subsequent generations. This is relevant to the concept of "The Inheritance."

27. Self-Efficacy: An individual's belief in their ability to succeed in specific situations or accomplish a task. This can be influenced by social conditioning and is important for personal growth.

28. Resilience: The capacity to recover quickly from difficulties; toughness. Understanding resilience can help in managing the impacts of social conditioning.

29. Social Learning Theory: The theory that people learn from one another, via observation, imitation, and modeling. This theory can provide additional insights into how social conditioning occurs.

30. Trauma-Informed Care: An approach in therapy and support services that involves understanding, recognizing, and responding to the effects of all types of trauma. This is especially relevant when addressing deep-seated conditioning from adverse childhood experiences.

31. **Self-Conditioning**: The process by which individuals unconsciously develop behavioral patterns and responses based on past experiences, often as survival mechanisms during childhood. These conditioned responses are created to protect oneself from perceived threats but may become maladaptive in adulthood, affecting relationships, emotional well-being, and overall life satisfaction. Recognizing and addressing self-conditioning is crucial for personal growth and healing.

Chapter 3 References

1. **Tajfel, H. (1981).** *Human Groups and Social Categories: Studies in Social Psychology.* **Cambridge University Press.**
- A foundational text on social psychology, exploring the impact of social categories on group behavior and identity. This book provides insights into how social conditioning operates through group dynamics and identity formation.

2. **Van der Kolk, B. (2014).** *The Body Keeps the Score: Brain, Mind, and Body in the Healing of Trauma.* **Viking.**
- This work explains how trauma impacts both the brain and body, offering insights into the long-term effects of childhood conditioning and the process of healing.

3. **Mischel, W. (2014).** *The Marshmallow Test: Why Self-Control Is the Engine of Success.* **Little, Brown, and Company.**
- Mischel's research on delayed gratification and self-control offers a deeper understanding of how early conditioning can influence long-term behaviors.

4. **Bandura, A. (1977).** *Social Learning Theory.* **Prentice-Hall.**
- This theory is key to understanding how individuals learn behaviors through observation and imitation, highlighting the role of social conditioning in behavior development.

5. **Schore, A. N. (2003).** *Affect Regulation and the Repair of the Self.* **Norton.**

- Schore's work delves into the neurological basis of emotional regulation, which is crucial in understanding the effects of childhood conditioning on adult behavior.

6. **Perry, B. D., & Szalavitz, M. (2006).** *The Boy Who Was Raised as a Dog: And Other Stories from a Child Psychiatrist's Notebook.* **Basic Books.**
- This book offers case studies that illustrate the profound impact of childhood trauma and conditioning, providing practical examples of healing and recovery.

7. **Felitti, V. J., Anda, R. F., et al. (1998).** *Relationship of Childhood Abuse and Household Dysfunction to Many of the Leading Causes of Death in Adults: The Adverse Childhood Experiences (ACE) Study.* **American Journal of Preventive Medicine, 14(4), 245-258.**
- The ACE study is a pivotal research project that links childhood experiences to adult health outcomes, emphasizing the long-term effects of early conditioning.

8. **Porges, S. W. (2011).** *The Polyvagal Theory: Neurophysiological Foundations of Emotions, Attachment, Communication, and Self-Regulation.* **Norton.**
- Porges' Polyvagal Theory provides a framework for understanding how the autonomic nervous system shapes emotional and social behavior, relevant to the discussion of conditioned responses.

9. **Damasio, A. (1999).** *The Feeling of What Happens: Body and Emotion in the Making of Consciousness.* **Harcourt Brace.**

- Damasio's exploration of consciousness and emotions offers insights into how our bodily experiences shape our emotional life and decision-making processes, linked to the effects of conditioning.

10. **Siegel, D. J. (2012).** *The Developing Mind: How Relationships and the Brain Interact to Shape Who We Are.* **Guilford Press.**
- This book examines the interplay between brain development and relationships, providing a deeper understanding of how early experiences influence social and emotional development.

11. **A special selection for Self-Conditioning.**
   1. **Van der Kolk, B. (2014). The Body Keeps the Score: Brain, Mind, and Body in the Healing of Trauma.** New York: Viking. This book explores how traumatic experiences can lead to ingrained behavioral responses, influencing self-conditioning.

   2. **Schwartz, A. (n.d.).** *Complex PTSD and Self-Conditioning.* This source discusses the impact of complex PTSD on self-conditioning, explaining how repeated exposure to stress or trauma leads to ingrained behavioral responses that persist into adulthood.

   3. **Levine, P. A. (1997).** *Waking the Tiger: Healing Trauma.* Berkeley, CA: North Atlantic Books. Levine's work provides insights into how trauma affects the body and mind, leading to self-conditioned responses that can be recognized and transformed through awareness and therapeutic techniques.

4. **Siegel, D. J. (2012).** *The Developing Mind: How Relationships and the Brain Interact to Shape Who We Are.* New York: Guilford Press. This book offers a deep understanding of how early relationships and experiences condition the brain and behavior, shedding light on the process of self-conditioning.

5. **Kabat-Zinn, J. (1990).** *Full Catastrophe Living: Using the Wisdom of Your Body and Mind to Face Stress, Pain, and Illness.* New York: Delacorte Press. This book discusses how mindfulness and self-awareness can help identify and recondition the automatic responses that develop over time, often in response to stress and trauma.

What's on your nose, you can't see it.

—Ali Najafi

Chapter Four
The Dual Nature of Self

We all have both light and dark sides. The light side encompasses our conscious thoughts and beliefs, where we see ourselves as good people doing good things. The dark side, however, consists of unconscious behaviors, thoughts, and feelings. This hidden side can dominate our lives because it operates without our awareness. Understanding this duality empowers us to work with both aspects of ourselves, leading to growth and self-awareness.

It's crucial to note that many good aspects of ourselves exist in the dark side. So, this isn't about good versus evil—it's about the seen and unseen. During the seven years I spent largely alone, getting to know myself, I found many parts of myself I liked but weren't being expressed around others. For example, I love the quietness of nature. I'm not a big planner, which lets me be spontaneous—something I've come to appreciate. I can be opinionated, but that doesn't make me judgmental; my opinions change as quickly as the wind.

The beauty of it is that these opinions don't define who I am; they're just fleeting parts of a whole, ever-changing self.

Understanding Triggers

When someone else's behavior triggers a strong emotional response in us, it often reflects an aspect of ourselves that needs attention. Instead of blaming the other person, use the trigger as a tool to explore your feelings and reactions.

For instance, if someone's anger triggers you, it might point to unresolved anger within yourself. Recognizing these reflections helps you understand your hidden emotions and behaviors. However, attracting angry people doesn't always mean you have unexpressed anger. I've gotten this feedback from so many people. There are numerous possibilities; it's up to you to narrow them down to find the root cause. When you say, "I keep attracting the same kind of people," it indicates a desire to change something within, particularly if they don't support your life, growth, or happiness.

Let's consider a simple trigger: an empty milk bottle left in the fridge. This doesn't necessarily mean you are unloved or unappreciated. It could mean that someone has never considered what happens when the milk runs out. If you feel unappreciated or unloved, this is a reflection of an internal state that you have created.

A friend once told me he had never thought about what happened to his dirty clothes after he tossed them in the hamper. They would magically reappear, clean and folded, in his dresser. Yes, he knew his mom did all this, but he had never considered what was involved between the hamper and the dresser until he had to do it himself. After that experience, he made sure to tell his mom how much he appreciated what she did for him.

Bringing it back to the milk: the person who sees the empty milk container thinks that the empty milk container is about themselves. Well, their reaction is about themselves and what they think they deserve. Now, the part about the deserves is why they feel bad. The anger they feel about it is that the other person triggered them to remember how they feel about themselves. By exploring this feeling, they can examine why they react this way.

Expecting the person who left the empty milk bottle in the fridge, to change so you don't have to experience your triggered emotions is never going to work. Trying to change the world so you don't have to feel bad is a defeatist plan. People are going to be who they are. If you nurture self-love, you won't be triggered because there won't be a trigger. We'll dive deeper into this concept as we go on.

Healthy Expression of Emotions

It's crucial to express negative emotions like anger in a healthy way to manage them effectively.

Until the constant expression of anger in TV series, anger was not considered an appropriate feeling to dump on other people. Within a few years of this happening on TV, people started to dump their anger freely everywhere.

Many times, anger is a result of our boundaries not being respected. And we don't even know it was about boundaries. We will get deeper into this in the next chapter.

To me, it is inappropriate to dump your anger on anyone. It is essential to identify with another person that you are feeling angry about a situation or their behavior or that you are angry but not at them. Identify it. Let them know you need time.

Walk it off. Run. Jump up and down while listening to fast, wild music. Scream into a pillow.

Your higher brain functioning is not available during anger. Or, it is at least dramatically reduced. Don't beat yourself or the dog or your partner or your child or anyone else that you are feeling anger towards. You will slowly calm down when you take time away from whatever made you angry. Once it dissipates, you will be able to use your brain again and look at the situation with fresher eyes.

This practice prevents drastic actions from making you regret them later. Techniques such as journaling, talking to a trusted friend, and engaging in physical activity can help release pent-up emotions. And, of course, having a therapist to work with if needed.

A Childhood Reflection

To highlight the importance of managing anger effectively, let me share a personal experience demonstrating uncontrolled anger's destructive potential. Trigger warning: There is violence in this story. If it triggers you, stop reading. Take a break and let it settle down. If you start again and are triggered, I suggest speaking to the therapist and telling them exactly what triggered you. And, of course, you don't have to read this part.

My mother and stepfather had a dynamic that was destructive in its perfection. She would berate and belittle him over something he said or did until he snapped. His eyes would glaze over, empty, as he lost control and began beating her.

The violence was brutal. She would end up on the floor, a bloody mess, unable to continue her verbal attacks because of the pain, her mouth full of blood. He would only stop once he realized what he was doing, then run off to the bedroom, crying in shame and self-loathing.

Slowly, she would pick herself up, cursing through the blood, grab her purse and car keys, and head to the hospital. Once patched up, she would return, still cursing as she came through the door. She would march to the bedroom, pack a suitcase, and yell, "You son of a bitch, see if I ever come back again!"

Can you imagine how all of this affected my sisters and me?

A week would go by, and my stepfather would be a mess, not knowing where she was or if she was ok. Sometimes, he would just be staring into space or suddenly, out of nowhere, crying intensely or screaming and yelling at us: my sisters and I.

After about a week, she would show up, planning to get more clothes. She would head to the bedroom, methodically going through the drawers. If he hadn't appeared by then, she would have neatly folded the clothes onto the bed.

Inevitably, he would suddenly rush into the room, throw himself on the floor, and beg her not to leave, promising never to do it again, all the while crying like a baby. This cycle continued from when I was two until I was fourteen, when my mother finally divorced him.

These repeated cycles of anger and violence were etched into my young mind, leaving me with a deep understanding of how unchecked emotions can destroy lives. However, they also ignited a determination within me—a drive to break this pattern and find healthier ways to cope with anger.

This experience taught me early on that when anger is left unchecked and allowed to spiral; it can cause irreversible harm to those we love. It reinforced the importance of finding healthy outlets for negative emotions and not allowing them to fester and explode.

This has been the most challenging of my emotional work. I swore early on that I would never hit a woman, but that vow wasn't enough. I struggled to express my anger healthily throughout three marriages. Now, I may finally be learning. In my current relationship, I can step back and give myself time until my triggers subside.

All I wanted was for my partner to understand why I felt the way I did. I didn't need to be right unless my partner made an effort to see and validate my feelings. If they didn't or couldn't, I would fall into helplessness, which triggered anger. The depth of this one is still being processed, but I no longer need the understanding that was so desperate inside me. Meditation and the work I have done with myself and others have helped me gain some distance from the issue. I have come to recognize that the first thing for me is that I am experiencing self-righteousness. Postponing this was key to my salvation from anger.

The cathartic experience of losing the love of my life, reconnecting with self-love, and spending seven years alone to get to know myself intimately has played a significant role in this growth.

Reflection and Projection

People in your life often mirror aspects of yourself, especially those you have repressed or are unaware of. For instance, if someone's anger triggers you, it might suggest unresolved anger within yourself. Recognizing these reflections helps you understand your hidden emotions and behaviors.

However, as I mentioned earlier, attracting angry people doesn't always mean you have unexpressed anger. There are many possibilities; you must narrow them down to find the root cause. When you say, "I keep attracting the same kind of people," it indicates a desire to change something within, notably if they don't support your life, growth, or happiness.

The Power of the Mind

This section holds the key to unlocking the most powerful tool you possess—the ability to recreate your life over and over again. By fully grasping the mind's role in shaping your reality, you'll gain access to the most profound transformation this book offers. Embrace it, and you will have the power to continually reshape your world.

Your mind is incredibly powerful, creating a reality that aligns with your unconscious beliefs. This means you attract people and situations that reflect your internal states. Understanding this concept is crucial because it empowers you to take responsibility for your experiences and use them as opportunities for growth. Recognize that you are the creator of your life, and by changing your beliefs, you can change your reality. Your reality is based upon what you think and feel about yourself subconsciously.

Be aware, however, that this subconscious realm often contains the 'dark side'—limiting beliefs and unresolved emotions—that, if left unchecked, will continue to shape your life in ways you might not consciously desire.

How the Subconscious Mind Creates Reality

The subconscious mind shapes your reality in a way that can be compared to creating a collage. This isn't a perfect analogy, but it can help illustrate the concept.

As you go through life, you start creating a 'collage' of pictures of people, places, and events on the walls of your subconscious mind. When I say pictures, I mean sensory impressions. This 'collage' creates an overall theme based on the total of what is on that wall—the most prevailing experiences. This forms your self-identity.

Over time, the subconscious selectively filters sensory input to align with the existing 'images' on this collage. For example, repeated exposure to negativity—such as verbal abuse or physical violence—leaves a significant mark. On the flip side, positive experiences, like a warm hug from a loved one, also contribute to this collage.

It's crucial to clarify that this isn't about conscious memory. Instead, it's about sensory impressions stored in parts of the brain that you can't access directly. Though most people are never taught how to interpret this communication, the subconscious mind continuously communicates with you, the resulting overall impression.

This collage includes both negative and positive experiences. However, again, the most predominant experiences define who you are subconsciously. If you constantly hear, "That's stupid." or "You're stupid," your subconscious belief will reflect that and create a reality.

These experiences on the collage were impressions that went beyond surface experiences, and not everything you experience goes onto the collage. Because of the subconscious's data limitations, it starts to select information that is relevant to what is already on the collage.

Then, the miraculous thing happens: <u>Your subconscious reaches out into the world and brings to you people, places, and things that match the theme of that collage.</u> It does this because it doesn't have direct communication with your conscious mind.

If this concept feels unclear, take a moment to reflect on it. Understanding this process is crucial.

Creating a New Reality

Your subconscious creates reality based on the collage's theme. It essentially asks, "This is what you think and feel about yourself—is this the reality you want?" This is how the subconscious communicates with you.

If you understand this and don't make your reality wrong or bad or think that the world is out to get you, you can look at it without judgment and see the changes you need to make. <u>That's all it's trying to do.</u> When you see it from this perspective, you can change your reality.

It gives you the power to change. You created this reality in the first place. It is yours. It belongs to you. It's not bad or good or right or wrong. It is just a reality. Then you can look at it and say, 'Well, this isn't exactly what I had in mind.'

You identify yourself as the conscious mind—the one with self-awareness, the one that rationalizes and relates to the idea that I am a good person trying to do good things—the part of you that has the real power to create your life.

Your reality is a collaboration between the conscious and subconscious mind!

Personal Reality

"And you will know the truth, and the truth will set you free."—*The Bible, John 8:32*

We each live in a personal reality, some aspects of which coincide with universal truths. Think of it as an external canvas where you create your masterpiece. It's not a literal Holodeck*, but it's a useful metaphor for how everything operates. This reality is like a program you can alter or modify at will.

The technique I just shared empowers you to change your life. Realize that you are the creator of your experiences and have the ability to change them. You are on a playground, free to create the life you desire within specific parameters. The people, places, and situations you encounter are all part of your creation. They are all a reflection of you and what you have created.

One of the pitfalls that a person can run into is that if I'm the creator of my life, I'm at fault for how it is. That is simultaneously true and not true. Let's look at it this way. You are not at fault for what you didn't know.

Also, we are taught growing up that there has to be someone to blame if something isn't good. If you notice when you look for who's at fault, then someone needs to be punished.

Do you have time to create change or heal if you are busy punishing yourself? In my life, when I was busy punishing or blaming myself, I didn't have time or space to heal or change. I threw away my fault-finding system long ago. It didn't serve me.

The techniques in this book are designed to change the "program" you're running. As you continue to modify your subconscious collage, your reality will change dramatically. Everything in this book is built around this principle: changing your beliefs about yourself will change the world you experience.

Practical Application

I have already given you the clue to changing your reality. It is inherent in the system. To implement these changes, focus on overwhelming the 'collage' in your subconscious with how you genuinely want to see yourself. It's crucial to approach this with honesty and clarity, not just through affirmations but through real-life experiences.

For example, a significant change I made in my own 'collage' was eliminating the habit of telling myself I was stupid. Instead of replacing it with the affirmation, "You are the most intelligent person I know," I simply stopped engaging in negative self-talk. Gradually, the negativity faded and was replaced by positive feedback I started to notice. People began complimenting me, such as saying, "I love how you can discuss such deep philosophical subjects." These compliments had been there all along, but my previous negative self-talk had overshadowed them.

When you catch yourself thinking or saying something negative, use a technique like, "Cancel that, please," to dismiss it. For instance, if you think, "That was so stupid. I don't know why I did that," repeating this can make it a self-fulfilling prophecy. Your mind tends to focus on what you create most. If you repeatedly label actions as stupid, your mind will unconsciously reinforce those actions. The sooner you eliminate negative self-talk, the quicker you'll see positive changes in your life.

Personally, I never think of myself as stupid, and I never say negative things to myself. I never even say them as some excuse or explanation of behavior. And if I perform an action that doesn't yield what I'm looking for, I examine the behavior and change it when I can. It takes vigilance in the beginning, but it will pay off.

Let's review: The subconscious mind creates a theme for your self-belief. It attracts people, places, and situations as a reality to show you what you have created for yourself. You are then given the opportunity to assess if this is the reality that you want to live in. Then, without judgment, If not, you modify the theme in the subconscious mind so it can regenerate a new reality for you. Once again, you can review it to see if it is correct. There is nothing good or bad about it. It is how the subconscious mind communicates with the conscious mind.

The conscious mind communicates back to the subconscious mind by flooding it with refined data about your desired reality. For example, you are sitting in front of a nice warm fire with the person you want to be with, and you feel loved and loving.

You consciously acknowledge everything in your environment, and you say to yourself, "More of this, please." Or, you can say, "I would like more of this or something better. Please." Why do I add the "Please"? It is respecting yourself and your creative process.

For addressing negative self-talk, use "Cancel that, please. What I meant to say is _____," replacing it with something positive.

Digressing again: I learned that little technique from Debra Poneman in her "Yes to Success" course many years ago. Thank you, Debra!

Final Thoughts

You might want to review this chapter. All the techniques building to this point and after this will always relate back to what you learned here. Remember, forgiveness, patience, and self-kindness are your vehicle to get you home.

You have always been creating your life; now you can start shaping it according to your true desires. My grandpa used to say, "If you don't have something nice to say about someone, don't say anything at all." I've taken that further by applying it to how I speak to myself.

If we can stop saying bad things about ourselves, we create an empty space that we can now fill with goodness and love. That might seem a little cheesy, but if you don't have any cheesy love for yourself, how are you going to have any for anyone else?

__Holodeck__, from the TV series "Star Trek, The Next Generation." A room that was programmed so you can experience things like lying on a beach or playing billiards in a pool hall, all while you are traveling through space. It was a simulated reality machine.

Glossary for Chapter 4: The Dual Nature of Self

1. **Dual Nature of Self**: The concept that individuals possess both a light side (conscious thoughts and beliefs) and a dark side (unconscious behaviors, thoughts, and feelings). This duality can influence actions and interactions.

2. **Triggers**: Events or behaviors that evoke a strong emotional response due to unresolved issues or past experiences. Recognizing triggers can help in managing reactions and understanding underlying issues.

3. **Healthy Expression of Emotions**: The practice of expressing emotions in a constructive and non-harmful way. This helps prevent the build-up of negative emotions and promotes emotional well-being.

4. **Reflection and Projection**: Reflection involves seeing aspects of oneself in others, while projection is the process of attributing one's own feelings or traits onto someone else. Understanding these concepts can help in recognizing unconscious patterns.

5. **The Power of the Mind**: The idea that our thoughts and beliefs shape our reality. The subconscious mind influences the experiences and people we attract, based on our internal state.

6. **Subconscious Mind**: The part of the mind that operates below the level of conscious awareness, storing beliefs, memories, and experiences that shape behavior and perception.

7. **Collage of Experiences**: A metaphor for the collection of significant memories and experiences stored in the subconscious mind. This collage influences one's beliefs and interactions.

8. **Personal Reality**: The unique way an individual perceives and experiences the world, shaped by their thoughts, feelings, and subconscious beliefs.

9. **Mindfulness**: The practice of being present and fully engaged with the current moment, observing thoughts and emotions without judgment. Mindfulness helps in recognizing and addressing subconscious patterns.

10. **Self-Awareness**: The conscious knowledge of one's own character, feelings, motives, and desires. Self-awareness is essential for recognizing the dual nature of the self and managing emotions.

11. **Introspection**: The examination of one's own thoughts and feelings.

12. Introspection aids in understanding unconscious patterns and behaviors.

13. **Shadow Work**: The process of exploring and integrating the unconscious parts of oneself, often referred to as the "shadow." Shadow work helps in achieving emotional balance and self-awareness.

14. **Cognitive Dissonance**: The mental discomfort experienced when holding two or more contradictory beliefs or values. Recognizing cognitive dissonance can aid in resolving inner conflicts.

15. **Self-Compassion**: Treating oneself with kindness and understanding, especially when dealing with the darker aspects of the self. Self-compassion is crucial for emotional healing and growth.

16. **Emotional Triggers**: Specific stimuli that evoke strong emotional reactions due to unresolved past experiences. Identifying and understanding these triggers can help in managing reactions constructively.

17. **Personal Transformation**: The process of significant change in one's beliefs, behaviors, and self-perception. Personal transformation often involves addressing both the light and dark sides of the self.

18. **Emotional Healing**: The process of acknowledging and addressing emotional wounds, allowing for recovery and personal growth. Emotional healing involves both self-awareness and self-compassion.

References for Chapter 4

Studies and Books

1. Human Groups and Social Categories by Henri Tajfel

This book explores social psychology and the relations and conflicts between social groups. Tajfel's work on social identity and categorization provides insights into how our unconscious beliefs and the environment influence our behavior and self-perception (Cambridge University Press).

2. The Marshmallow Test by Walter Mischel

This classic experiment studied delayed gratification and its long-term effects on success. Mischel's findings highlight how early behavioral conditioning can shape our future behaviors and achievements, emphasizing the power of the subconscious mind (Verywell Mind).

3. Self and Society: Narcissism, Collectivism, and the Development of Morals

This book discusses the intellectual history of social thought and examines the nature of human behavior, providing a deeper understanding of self-concept and social conditioning within societal structures (Cambridge University Press).

4. Principles of Social Psychology: The Self

This module covers self-schemas, self-perception, and possible selves, explaining how our self-concept is formed and influenced by past experiences and social interactions (Open Text WSU).

Videos

1. The Social Dilemma (Netflix)

This documentary explores the impact of social networking on human behavior, showing how algorithms and psychological manipulation shape our subconscious beliefs and actions.

2. The Power of Social Influence by TEDx Talks

This video discusses various experiments and real-life examples that illustrate the power of social influence on individual behavior, highlighting the mechanisms of social conditioning.

3. Understanding Social Conditioning by Academy of Ideas

This video delves into the mechanisms of social conditioning and how it affects our beliefs and behaviors, providing practical insights into breaking free from societal constraints.

"Between the ears and eyes there lie the sounds of color,

and the light of a sigh."

The Moody Blues, *"The Word"*, from the album

In Search of the Lost Chord (1968)

Chapter Five
Boundaries

Between the ears and eyes, we navigate a world of unspoken communication—where emotions and thoughts, much like colors and sounds, are perceived and interpreted. Boundaries, though often invisible, are as real as the light of a sigh, shaping our interactions with the world and with each other. When we honor these boundaries, we honor the spaces where we exist as individuals, respecting the lines that connect and separate us.

Understanding Boundaries

Establishing and understanding boundaries is crucial for maintaining healthy relationships and personal well-being. Boundaries define the limits of acceptable behavior, protecting our mental, emotional, and physical space. According to Dr. Henry Cloud and Dr. John Townsend in their book *Boundaries*, healthy boundaries are essential for personal well-being and relationships. They describe a continuum where boundaries can be overly rigid, leading to isolation, or too permeable, resulting in being taken advantage of. Recognizing where we fall on this continuum helps us adjust and create healthier boundaries.

The Importance of Boundaries

Boundaries protect us, helping us maintain our sense of self and prevent others from encroaching on our personal space. They are essential for fostering respect and understanding in relationships, allowing us to communicate our needs and expectations.

Types of Boundaries

Different types of boundaries serve various purposes in our lives:

1. **Physical Boundaries**: These involve personal space and physical touch. Respecting physical boundaries means understanding and honoring an individual's comfort level with proximity and physical contact.

2. **Emotional Boundaries**: These protect our emotional well-being by allowing us to regulate our feelings and maintain emotional stability. Emotional boundaries help us avoid being overwhelmed by others' emotions and prevent emotional manipulation.

3. **Mental Boundaries**: These involve our thoughts, beliefs, and values. Mental boundaries allow us to maintain our individuality and intellectual autonomy, ensuring our opinions and ideas are respected.

4. **Material Boundaries**: These pertain to our possessions and resources. Material boundaries help us manage our belongings and financial resources, preventing others from exploiting our generosity.

5. **Time Boundaries**: These involve how we allocate our time and energy. Time boundaries help us prioritize our commitments and avoid overextending ourselves.

Experiencing Your Boundaries

You can feel an actual physiological and emotional experience of boundaries. Here's how you can feel yours: Have the closest person you know stand about 7 or 8 feet away from you, just standing there looking at one another. Notice how you feel emotionally and physically. Then, have them step closer.

Pay attention to your reactions with each step. You will likely feel a growing urge to push them away or create distance as they come closer. If you find yourself very close, you either have a strong trust in them or very flexible boundaries. Even with trust, it's important to know when to allow closeness and when to need more distance. Try this exercise with someone you barely know to see how it affects you. This practice helps you understand and feel your boundaries.

Establishing and Maintaining Boundaries

Setting and maintaining boundaries requires self-awareness and assertiveness. Here are some steps to help you set healthy boundaries:

1. **Identify Your Limits**: Reflect on your needs and values to determine your boundaries. Consider what makes you feel comfortable and what causes you stress or discomfort.

2. **Communicate Clearly**: Express your boundaries assertively and respectfully. Use "I" statements to convey your needs and avoid blaming or criticizing others.

3. **Be Consistent**: Enforce your boundaries consistently to reinforce their importance. Consistency helps others understand and respect your limits.

4. **Respect Others' Boundaries**: Just as you expect others to respect your boundaries, be mindful of theirs. Mutual respect fosters healthy and balanced relationships.

5. **Adjust Your Boundaries**: Adjust your boundaries according to your situation. Over time, this will become

very intuitive. Good boundaries automatically remove you from situations with people you don't want or need. Victimizers are always unconsciously looking for victims. Victims are people who don't have boundaries or have fragile boundaries.

6. **Seek Support**: If establishing or maintaining boundaries is challenging, seek support from trusted friends, family members, or a therapist with healthy boundaries. They can provide valuable feedback, guidance, and encouragement.

Personal Experience with Boundaries

Boundaries have played a crucial role in both my personal and professional life. Setting and maintaining them has been essential for navigating relationships with clarity and confidence.

One experience stands out:

When I first started coaching, I found it challenging to establish boundaries with my clients. I wanted to be accessible and supportive, often leading to burnout and frustration. Over time, I learned the importance of setting clear boundaries to protect my well-being and maintain the quality of my coaching.

Holding courses at my retreat center put me in the middle of people's processes. Living there made it easy for guests to find me. They would sometimes show up in the morning while I was having coffee. Most of the time, it was not a problem. But sometimes, I just wanted to space out and drink my coffee and have useless and unproductive conversations with my wife.

One night, I was rudely woken up at 2:30 am by a loud pounding on the door. Thinking something was terribly wrong, I dragged my sleeping body to the door. A guest had just had a breakthrough and needed to share it. I listened for about 10 minutes, congratulated them, and returned them to their room. That was the last night that ever happened. The guests kept pushing over time what they could and couldn't have from me regarding time and expertise.

That night marked a turning point. I set my boundaries clearly, and from then on, interactions became much smoother. I also noticed that guests were significantly more respectful of my time without any additional effort on my part beyond setting those boundaries. My value to them increased as a result.

By clearly communicating my availability and limits, I created a balanced environment that benefited my students and myself in many ways. This experience taught me the value of boundaries in fostering healthy and sustainable relationships.

Three Stories About Boundaries

Consider these three scenarios about boundaries. Reflect on your reactions—not how you think you should react, but how you genuinely would. Write down your responses to each situation. There are no right or wrong answers; these scenarios are meant to help you explore how you interact with others.

1. **Scenario 1**: It's the weekend, and you're out at an event where you meet someone you get along with well. You spend most of the day together and invite them over for dinner the next day. You cook or buy a meal and set the table. As you're preparing, they arrive and you ask them to sit in the living room while you finish setting up. You suddenly hear them turn on your stereo. How do you feel about that?

2. **Scenario 2**: This is the same scenario, except this one has no stereo. You set the table, and they come into the kitchen and ask you where the bathroom is. You proceed

to tell them, and they leave the kitchen. Soon, you finish setting the table and go into the living room to invite them to the kitchen for dinner. They aren't there. You look down the hallway, and the bathroom door is open, and you see they are not there. You proceed to walk down the hallway, and you see they are in your bedroom. They are not doing anything, just looking around. How do you feel about that?

3. **Scenario 3**: You live in an apartment at the top of a staircase, sharing the space with a friend who lives next door. Usually, you leave the doors open between apartments, borrowing small items from each other without much formality. One day, while you're in the shower, your friend comes over to borrow $100. When they see you're in the shower, they notice your wallet on the coffee table, take a $100 bill from it, and leave. Later, you realize the $100 is missing when you're at the store. After searching your apartment and finding nothing, you manage with a makeshift meal. The next day, your friend returns with $100, thanking you for the loan. How do you feel?

Share these scenarios with close friends or someone you admire and compare responses. What did you learn through these stories?

Final Thoughts

Boundaries are vital for maintaining healthy relationships and personal well-being. Understanding and establishing boundaries can protect our mental, emotional, and physical space, ensuring our needs and values are respected. Embrace the process of setting boundaries as a journey towards self-awareness and empowerment.

A phenomenon often occurs with healthy boundaries: what I refer to as "Holding Space." When I managed the retreat center, I was responsible for creating and maintaining a safe environment. This served two main purposes:

1. It provided a sense of security. Guests felt that the retreat was a special place where they could explore their needs and make necessary changes in their lives.

2. It involved safeguarding the space from unwanted intrusions. Unlike other resorts in the area, which faced issues like theft and unsafe situations, our center remained secure.

To understand this concept better, imagine yourself in a serene, quiet space, completely undisturbed. Close your eyes gently, take a deep breath, and let your mind clear. Visualize an invisible wall surrounding you. This boundary might not be immediately clear, but with patience, allow it to form in your mind. For some, it may appear as a translucent bubble of soft light; for others, a more solid, transparent barrier.

Picture yourself outside of your body for a moment, gently approaching this boundary. Observe its texture—perhaps it's smooth, maybe it glows faintly with a bluish hue. Stay present until you can clearly feel and see it surrounding you.

Once you've visualized this boundary fully, practice holding it in your awareness. Sit with this image, allowing it to become comfortable and familiar, like a protective space. Recognize that this is *your* space, and nothing can come into it without your consent. The bubble is strong and flexible, capable of expanding and contracting as needed, always under your control.

Now, imagine this bubble expanding—a slow, deliberate growth. Watch as it stretches, first to the edges of the room you're in. As you hold this space, feel the energy within it—strong, secure, and balanced. Nothing can enter this space unless you choose to allow it.

Once this becomes natural, expand further. Imagine your boundary now encompassing the entire building you're in, stretching out effortlessly. You are still at its center, calmly aware of the space you hold. Only those you permit can share in this space, and nothing can cross its threshold without your invitation.

When you're ready, continue to let it grow. Envision it moving outward, gently covering the street, then your neighborhood, and further still—your town, your city. With each expansion, pause to hold the boundary, feeling its strength and integrity.

Expand the bubble outward as far as you can—your state, your country, and even the entire world—while remaining present with the sensation of holding this vast space. Throughout, remind yourself that you are in control, and what enters this space requires your explicit consent.

Finally, reverse the process. Gradually contract the boundary from the world back to your country, town, street, building, room, and ultimately, to yourself. Sit with it at this close, comfortable range, knowing that you have the power to hold your space and maintain your boundaries while respecting those of others.

And for those wondering, "Does this make me invincible?" The answer is no. However, combined with the teachings of this book, this practice will help you lead a better and happier life.

Glossary for Chapter 5: Boundaries

1. **Boundaries**: Personal limits that define acceptable behavior and protect our mental, emotional, and physical space. Boundaries help maintain a sense of self and prevent others from encroaching on our personal space.

2. **Physical Boundaries**: Limits related to personal space and physical touch. Respecting physical boundaries means understanding and honoring an individual's comfort level with proximity and physical contact.

3. **Emotional Boundaries**: Limits that protect our emotional well-being by allowing us to regulate our feelings and maintain emotional stability. Emotional boundaries help avoid being overwhelmed by others' emotions and prevent emotional manipulation.

4. **Mental Boundaries**: Limits related to our thoughts, beliefs, and values. Mental boundaries allow us to maintain our individuality and intellectual autonomy, ensuring that our opinions and ideas are respected.

5. **Material Boundaries**: Limits concerning our possessions and resources. Material boundaries help manage our belongings and financial resources, preventing others from taking advantage of our generosity.

6. **Time Boundaries**: Limits on how we allocate our time and energy. Time boundaries help prioritize our commitments and avoid overextending ourselves.

7. **Self-Awareness**: The conscious knowledge of one's own character, feelings, motives, and desires. It involves being mindful of one's boundaries and understanding their importance.

8. **Assertiveness**: The quality of being self-assured and confident without being aggressive. Assertiveness

involves clearly expressing one's boundaries and needs while respecting others.

9. **Consistency**: The practice of enforcing boundaries regularly and reliably. Consistency helps reinforce the importance of boundaries and ensures they are respected.

10. **Respect**: The consideration and appreciation of others' boundaries and needs. Mutual respect fosters healthy and balanced relationships.

11. **Boundary Violation**: Occurs when someone crosses or disregards another person's boundaries, leading to discomfort, stress, or emotional harm.

12. **Therapist**: A trained professional who can help individuals establish and maintain healthy boundaries, providing guidance and support through therapeutic techniques.

13. **Self-Compassion**: Treating oneself with kindness and understanding, especially when establishing and maintaining boundaries. Self-compassion helps in upholding boundaries without feeling guilty or selfish.

14. **Boundary Setting**: The process of defining and communicating one's boundaries to others. It involves identifying personal limits and expressing them clearly and assertively.

15. **Boundary Maintenance**: The ongoing practice of upholding and reinforcing one's boundaries. It involves being consistent and assertive in protecting personal limits.

16. **Boundary Adjustment**: The process of revisiting and modifying boundaries as needed to accommodate changes in relationships or circumstances. It involves

being flexible and adaptive while maintaining core personal limits.

References for Chapter 5: Boundaries

Here are some relevant studies, books, and videos from sociology, psychology, and social anthropology to support the concepts discussed in Chapter Five: Boundaries:

Studies and Books

1. Cloud, H., & Townsend, J. (1992). *Boundaries: When to Say Yes, How to Say No to Take Control of Your Life*. Zondervan.

2. The Study of Boundaries Across the Social Sciences by Michèle Lamont and Virág Molnár. This comprehensive study examines the concept of boundaries within anthropology, sociology, and social psychology. It discusses how boundaries affect relational processes, social identity, and cultural mechanisms for boundary production. This is useful for understanding the theoretical underpinnings of personal boundaries in social contexts (Annual Review of Sociology).

3. *Ethnic Identities and Boundaries: Anthropological, Psychological, and Sociological Perspectives*. This work explores the formation of boundaries in ethnic identities and how these boundaries impact social interactions and group dynamics. It provides insight into how boundaries function at both individual and group levels (Oxford Research Encyclopedia).

4. *Self and Society: Narcissism, Collectivism, and the Development of Morals*. This book delves into the development of self-concept and boundaries within societal frameworks. It offers a historical perspective on social thought and the role of boundaries in shaping personal and collective identities (Cambridge University Press).

Videos

1. **The Importance of Boundaries** by TEDx Talks. This video discusses the critical role boundaries play in personal and professional relationships. It includes practical advice on how to establish and maintain healthy boundaries.

2. **Setting Healthy Boundaries** by Psych2Go. This video provides an overview of the different types of boundaries and practical tips for maintaining them. It emphasizes the psychological benefits of setting clear boundaries in various aspects of life.

3. **Understanding Personal Boundaries** by Academy of Ideas. This video explores the concept of personal boundaries from a philosophical and psychological perspective, highlighting their importance in maintaining mental and emotional well-being.

Emotional Healing in Action

(This is an AI rendition of a photograph taken on one of the courses we offered at the retreat center.)

Chapter Six
Emotional Healing

Carl Rogers, a pioneer in humanistic psychology, emphasized the importance of offering oneself unconditional positive regard—an attitude of complete acceptance and understanding without self-judgment. This principle plays a crucial role in emotional healing and personal growth. By practicing self-acceptance, we create a space where we can process and release emotions constructively, allowing for deeper emotional well-being.

Understanding and addressing emotional wounds is a vital step in the journey toward self-discovery and healing. Emotional healing involves:

1. Acknowledging past traumas.

2. Understanding their impact on our current behavior and feelings.

3. Taking steps to heal and move forward.

The Nature of Emotional Wounds

Emotional wounds can stem from various sources, including childhood experiences, relationships, and significant life events. These wounds often shape our beliefs, behaviors, and interactions with others, sometimes leading to patterns that hinder our growth and well-being.

Recognizing Emotional Wounds

The first step in emotional healing is recognizing and acknowledging these wounds. This process involves self-reflection and an honest assessment of our past and present experiences. Signs of unhealed emotional wounds may include recurring negative emotions, difficulty in relationships, and self-destructive behaviors.

Steps to Emotional Healing

1. Self-awareness: Cultivate an awareness of your emotions and the triggers that evoke strong reactions. Journaling and mindfulness practices can help you recognize patterns and understand the root causes of your emotional responses.

Understanding that many behaviors initially developed as survival mechanisms can help you start the healing process. In adulthood, these behaviors may become detrimental to our happiness and growth. We also develop behaviors based on self-beliefs, which are often unconscious. When examining nonproductive behaviors, it's useful to explore the emotions or feelings that accompany them.

For instance, heavy drinking might lead to feelings of shame or guilt the next day, which could, in an unconscious way, fulfill an emotional expectation. (Note: This perspective does not apply to those struggling with alcoholism, who face unique challenges and require different approaches.)

Recognize that you made a choice regarding the behavior, and the resulting emotion stems from that choice. Instead of judging yourself harshly, approach the situation with neutrality. This allows for exploration of why you acted as you did. Curiosity can uncover the core self-beliefs that might have driven you to seek that emotional payoff.

2. Acceptance: Accept your emotions without judgment. Allow yourself to feel and process your feelings rather than suppressing or ignoring them. You may not be able to accept them when you are deep in them.

Remember, emotions have this sense of universality or all-pervasiveness. The mind is running, trying to support the idea that they are there forever. But with intention, you can lessen the depth of the emotion and the length of time it lasts. As soon as you know, you can accept it, do that, and know it will transition to something else.

3. Forgiveness: Forgive yourself and others for past hurts. Forgiving does not mean condoning harmful behavior but instead releasing the hold that past pain has on your present life.

4. Seeking Support: Reach out to trusted friends, family members, or a therapist. There are also good support groups for this. Sharing your experiences and feelings with others can provide comfort and perspective.

5. Healing Practices: Engage in activities that promote healing and self-care, such as meditation, creative expression, and physical exercise. These practices help release emotional tension and foster a sense of well-being. Additionally, you may meet others experiencing similar changes.

An Example of Emotional Healing in Action

A woman I worked with once came to me because she kept attracting men who would physically abuse her. At the time, she was fleeing her home because a former boyfriend—whom she had sent to prison—was about to be released and had threatened to kill her.

She hoped for two things when she came to me:

1. **Stay out of his way:** She wanted to avoid him until he settled down or violated his parole so he would return to prison.

2. **Understand her pattern:** She sought to uncover why she was drawn to such men.

I was giving a talk one day on her course on how Human beings are mammals. Therefore, parents love their children, and children love their parents. They have no choice.

She interrupted me and said, "I have a choice. I hate my father. When I left home, I never saw him again, and I will never see that man in this lifetime. I have no love for him."

She went on later to confide in me what he had done to her since she was 13 years old. This happened often, and she got out of there as soon as she was old enough.

"Someone like this doesn't deserve to be loved!" She said.

I proceeded to ask her again why she was here on the course.

"Because I attract men that abuse me." She said. I asked her, how many of them beat you and raped you or had violent sex with you?

She responded, "All of them. I don't know love. I have never had a partner that truly loved me."

After this, I spoke with her in a session. I suggested, "Maybe you're still holding onto something from him. What if, deep down, a part of you still loves him? It doesn't mean you have to forgive or reconnect. But accepting that love, simply because he's your father, might allow you to move forward."

She reacted with intense anger. "I hate you! I hate him! I'll never accept that!" she shouted through tears. She locked herself in her room, crying for hours. It was a deep release. By evening, her crying shifted, and she came to talk again.

"I found it," she said. "I found my love for my father. I always loved him, even though I hated him for what he did. And because I couldn't face that love, I buried it. But now I see how I kept attracting men like him, trying to heal that wound."

She expressed the freedom she felt after realizing this inner conflict. "For years, I loathed myself for loving him. But after today, the pain is gone. The memory remains, but it's not weighing me down anymore."

We discussed her next steps, and I encouraged her to process her emotions with a therapist without needing to confront or reconcile with her father unless she felt ready or even wanted to.

She called me sometime after she left and shared that her ex-boyfriend had been sent to prison for violating parole—another unhealthy relationship she had now distanced herself from. She was healing and dating men completely different from those she'd previously attracted.

Primal Therapy

Trigger warning: Primal Therapy should always be conducted under professional supervision. It's a powerful technique, and without proper guidance, especially if you're dealing with significant emotional trauma, it can lead to unforeseen complications.

At the retreat center, one of the techniques we frequently used was Primal Therapy. This method is particularly useful when you feel stuck and recognize that some emotions need to be released.

It involves a metal baseball bat, a secluded place, a huge rock, and goggles. A hat can be handy for long hair, and gloves help prevent blisters and vibrations. The intention is to beat the hell out of the rock with all your might while screaming at the top of your lungs.

You can focus on the beating of the rock as someone with whom you have unresolved deep emotional feelings. You beat them (the rock) with all your might and scream at them what you have never said before or what you feel needs to be said. It is an excellent way of releasing pent-up anger that has never been expressed with such purpose and intensity.

You continue with this until it is all out. Maybe It wasn't just one person, or it was you with whom you had anger. We all know it isn't a good idea to take a baseball bat and beat someone we are angry with. But a big rock or boulder can handle it. I don't suggest a tree because it is too alive, and you may be unable to let go. And, if you are a little worried about the rock, you can put your hand on it and ask if it is willing to take your frustration and anger. Everyone who did this at the retreat center got a clear "Yes or No" in their head.

The impact of this therapy was also notable among others at the retreat center. Witnessing someone's intense release often inspired onlookers, who would cheer them on. Participants who started the process looking timid or tearful would return from the hilltop visibly transformed—exhausted, emotional, but also liberated and happy. I would always have them report back to me to gauge their state, and while occasionally someone needed another round, this method generally proved effective.

You may be wondering why we used a metal baseball bat. We started with axe handles and wooden baseball bats. They wouldn't last an entire session without being destroyed. Sending someone up there with four or five wooden baseball bats got expensive fast and was a lot to carry up.

If you decide to try this, ensure that your baseball bat doesn't bounce excessively upon hitting a solid surface—being struck by a bouncing bat is dangerous. Additionally, it's advisable to have someone nearby who you can talk to afterward. It's best to be alone while performing the therapy, but having someone close can provide support if needed.

We once had a couple where, during her session on the hilltop, he heard her scream his name a few times. While we were having lunch, his reaction was one of surprise. Afterward, he was notably kinder to her. She emerged from the experience assertive and changed. As far as I know, they didn't discuss it, but the experience clearly had a lasting impact.

Personal Experience with Emotional Healing

Before We Begin:

As you read through this story, I encourage you to have a pen and paper handy. You might find certain parts resonate with you, or maybe you'll notice a pattern or emotion that feels familiar. I want you to create a space to jot down your reflections and make note of anything that stands out to you. By the end of this exercise, you might even have the beginning of your own story of transformation.

Emotional healing has been a significant part of my journey. One experience, in particular, stands out:

For a long time, I was very reactive in relationships. My response was always about me and my feelings in an argument. I interpreted my partner's behavior as something about me, so I would react without thinking about what had just happened.

Key Point: In emotional situations, our initial reaction often centers around ourselves. Recognizing this tendency allows for deeper self-reflection.

I recall a moment in the kitchen of our retreat center, where my wife was preparing lunch for our guests. During our discussion, she said something that hurt my feelings, and I responded with anger. The tension had been building all morning, and I felt her comment was unjust. From my wounded perspective, I retorted with a sharp remark.

Key Point: Emotional triggers can quickly escalate a situation if we don't pause to consider what's happening on both sides.

The discussion escalated from there. She retaliated, and we exchanged barbs, until I finally left the kitchen to calm down. When I cooled off, I thought, "How did this argument escalate so quickly? I want to understand this."

Key Point: Curiosity about our reactions can open the door to deeper understanding and change.

The next thing I knew, I was mentally walking through the discussion step by step. I focused on my breathing to stay grounded and not get caught up in the emotions. When the scenario played out in my mind, I asked myself, "What did you notice?"

I immediately felt the hurt from her comment, and my mind began pulling in past experiences where she had hurt me. It was like a flood of memories reinforcing the belief that she often wounded me and that I was never truly understood.

Key Point: Our minds tend to connect current emotional experiences with past wounds, which can magnify our reactions.

I stopped myself from spiraling into the familiar pit of despair and hurt. This time, I asked, "Let's review this again, but not from my position. Could there be another truth?"

Key Point: Taking a step back and seeing things from a different perspective can shift how we interpret the situation.

This time, I noticed how both of us were hurting each other. I started to feel her pain, which I hadn't acknowledged before. As I sat with this realization, I became aware that my usual reaction was to focus solely on my own pain.

Key Point: Recognizing your partner's pain as well as your own brings more balance to understanding the situation.

Then, the thought came: "Actually, I love her and don't want to hurt her." This was a significant shift for me. From there, I reviewed the situation again, but this time more slowly. When I played it out, I realized she hadn't said what I thought she had. She had been complimenting me on something I did.

Key Point: Misinterpretations of what someone says can easily happen in emotionally charged moments. Slowing down and reviewing can reveal the truth.

I checked it out with her, and sure enough, she confirmed that she had been complimenting me. I was the one who misinterpreted her words.

We sat down to discuss what had happened. Both of us shared how we saw the pattern playing out in our relationship, how I often interpreted her comments as criticism, and how she felt misunderstood.

Key Point: Open communication after an argument helps uncover deeper patterns that may be driving the conflict.

Through this process, I discovered that a childhood belief made me seek out situations where I felt discredited. She had her own unresolved issues related to feeling misunderstood and unfairly criticized. We both committed to working on these underlying beliefs.

Key Point: Emotional reactions often stem from childhood beliefs, and recognizing this can help heal deep-seated patterns.

In time, we argued less and learned to communicate better. I began to check in with her before jumping to conclusions about what she meant, which helped us avoid unnecessary conflict.

Key Point: Cultivating the habit of checking in with your partner can prevent future misunderstandings and reduce conflicts.

The Impact of Parental Influence

Let's address the influence of parent-child interactions. Parents get a pretty bad rap when it comes to our personal growth. A lot of techniques make the parents out to be bad people. They messed us up. It is their fault. Well, there is no right or wrong or good or bad when it comes to raising children. No one gave us a manual on how to raise children. And no one gave our parents a manual. I'm not talking about some book written by a psychologist about children. I mean a genuine child-rearing operator manual. You know, like the one you got with your new car, TV, or stereo.

Natural vs Normal

In my lifetime, I've observed this distinction: natural human behavior is inherently unpredictable, while normal human behavior is remarkably predictable.

A natural human being operates without constraints from behavioral issues, ideally raised in a nurturing, supportive environment by parents who are also free from significant behavioral issues and have ample time to dedicate to their children.

In contrast, a normal human being is more representative of you, me, and nearly everyone around us.

If you have a negative internal belief, then you can rest assured that other people have the same belief. It doesn't matter if someone is physically beaten into this belief or psychologically or emotionally beaten into it. Your behaviors will be very similar. The differences will vary slightly due to economic or social background.

Consider the brain and nervous system as both highly sophisticated and, at the same time, quite simple. We possess consciousness, emotions, and thoughts, yet we also respond on a fundamental level to basic stimuli. The nervous system reacts to external and internal inputs, though it isn't conscious itself—it merely responds. Pain, whether physical, psychological, or emotional, impacts the nervous system similarly, leading to inflammation and changes in behavior.

Now, here's something you might not expect: Ask a torture specialist about pain, and they'll tell you—pain is pain. It doesn't matter if it's physical, emotional, or psychological; the nervous system reacts in similar ways. This is why all three forms of abuse are used in torture—because they each achieve the same goal, breaking down the nervous system's defenses and affecting the mind.

To be clear, I am not equating our parents with torture specialists!

Knowing this can give you the ability to have empathy or compassion for someone who was emotionally abused as a child if you were, say, physically abused. The behavioral changes are very similar.

A natural human being will respond to any given situation to the absolute highest possible outcome for everyone affected by it. Humans are unpredictable, and you will not always see their behavior as appropriate and necessary at that time. They may not even know what the outcome will be.

As we grow and get closer to this natural state in our healing process, we can spontaneously fall into being "natural" occasionally. Here is an example of what I mean.

Early in my career, it became apparent that within any profession, there's a state of being I refer to as the "natural human state." We all experience this, though we might not be conscious of it. A spiritual teacher once called it the "working mind." This is the mind that analyzes and solves problems with ease, without much interference from what I call the "thinking mind."

For instance, when solving a math problem, the mind naturally navigates through the steps to reach a solution. The same applies to programming challenges or writing a novel where you guide a character from point A to point B. The mind generates possibilities and directs you toward the solution with minimal conscious effort.

If I step back and allow this natural state to operate unobstructed, the results can seem miraculous. I will share some of these experiences in this book.

The Natural Mind at Work

Before a morning session with a group I was leading, a woman not enrolled in the course approached me. She was upset because some participants had been loud into the night, speaking across their verandas, which kept her awake. I promised to address the issue and brought it up during our meeting.

Usually, I am a very patient person, and I don't get upset about these things, especially during a course meeting. But I noticed that I was very irritated. So, I began talking with the parties involved, and it was evident that I was upset about it. I asked myself what was going on, and I felt like I was sitting on the side to watch. I was used to this experience, but it was different from how it happened then. But not when I had an emotional reaction to something. So, I sat internally in observation of what was happening.

One of the course participants had an eating disorder and had come because she had been hospitalized three times because of it. She had been with me previously just because she was on holiday and heard about my work.

She had been with me for a week and made good progress. At the end of that week, I told her that if she were to be hospitalized again for her eating disorder, she should immediately come to me and stay for a month as soon as she was released from the hospital.

She agreed with me and soon after she went home. She did well for a short time and then fell right back into her eating disorder and was once again hospitalized. She called me as soon as she was released, got the next flight she could take, and arrived at the retreat center within a couple of days. She was, at this point, three weeks into her course. She had made significant progress but still had not gotten to the source of the disorder.

So here we were that morning, at odds with each other, and she was trying to explain to me why this all happened, and I would just cut her off in the middle of her explanations. She would try to explain to me, and I would cut her off and talk to one of the others who were a part of this evening of sleep interruption for another guest. All the time, I was talking to one of the others, and I was watching her.

She was pushing it down and trying to get my attention. Every time she did, I cut her off and talked to someone else. I noticed that all the while I was talking to someone else, she was my focus of attention, but she didn't know that.

Eventually, overwhelmed by my interruptions, she lost control and began crying hysterically—a reaction I had never encountered from her before. Known for my patience and empathy, I was surprised by my own irritation, especially since the issue seemed minor.

She yelled at me through her tears and attempted to leave. I told her it was okay to be angry but that she could not leave the retreat center until she had calmed down and spoken with me. She yelled at me that I didn't listen to her and was not doing anything to help her. She was fed up with everything, and she was leaving.

She stormed off to her bungalow, continuing to cry and yell.

The rest of the group was visibly shocked. Many felt I had been unsympathetic and dismissive. As my irritation dissipated, we resumed the session as though nothing had occurred.

About an hour later, a participant from that night knocked on my door, concerned for her well-being. She was locked in her room, crying and expressing a desire to die. I accompanied him to her bungalow, asking him to wait on his veranda for support if needed.

I approached her door, speaking softly as though addressing a wounded child. My tone was kind and gentle, not condescending. After some time, I asked if I could enter. She responded from beneath the bed, saying she wouldn't come out to unlock the door.

"I have a master key," I told her, "but I won't use it unless you let me."

We continued to talk back and forth. Her voice shook with pain, and I explained that it was hard for me to hear her through the door. Finally, she gave me permission to unlock it.

Once inside, I saw her. I found her wedged under the bed, which had barely six inches of clearance. I was astonished by how she managed to fit there. I initially sat on the other side of the room, giving her space. Slowly, her hysterical crying subsided, and she allowed me to lie down on the floor beside the bed. From that position, I spoke to her gently, just as I had before, while she expressed her anger.

"You interrupted me so many times. It made me feel like you didn't care about me," she said. "I trusted you, but now I feel lost."

Her words hit hard. I told her the truth—that I had never done that with anyone before. Not with a guest. Not even with a friend.

I told her, "I think we are close to what caused your eating disorder."

I asked her about her anger, and she said she rarely was angry. Then I asked her if she had ever experienced in her life previously that someone would interrupt her like I had in that meeting.

Suddenly, she broke down again into hysterical crying. I waited patiently, half squeezed under the bed so we could be eye to eye with each other. She cried and cried, and as she did, she said repeatedly.

"I don't know! I don't know!" She cried.

Suddenly, she completely stopped; her eyes widened, and she stammered.

"Myyyy–myyyy parents!" She cried.

"They would never let me speak. They would always interrupt me. They always told me to shut up. They always treated me like I didn't exist."

"I kept thinking, to them, they believe I shouldn't exist."

Now, my eyes filled with tears. "I think we have found it I said." Now, we both cried. But this time, she wasn't hysterically crying.

I asked her if I could hug her, recognizing the significant breakthrough she had made. We emerged from under the bed, and I held her in my arms like a father comforting his child. I spoke to her about the importance of her being there, expressing how much it meant to me and everyone else.

I helped her embrace that little girl inside of her who felt she shouldn't exist. Together, we assured that little girl that we loved her and wanted her around. Right then and there, she made a commitment to that little girl that she would always be there for her, that she wanted her with her, and that she would take care of her.

In that hour, cramped under that bed, she left that eating disorder there on the floor of that bungalow. She got up and walked away from it and never turned back.

She returned home to her fiancee, got married, and now has two beautiful children of her own.

I would never have predicted that my behavior would catalyze what happened that day. I never doubt my actions when working with clients. I never interfere with their process.

That was being a natural human being.

Conclusion

You can't expect automatic, permanent change. The process requires ongoing effort and self-awareness. Change may come swiftly or take days, weeks, or months. Vigilance and self-observation are crucial. Emotional healing is a continuous journey.

By acknowledging and addressing our wounds, we can transform pain into strength and wisdom. Embrace the journey of emotional healing as a path to greater self-awareness and empowerment. Sometimes, when you step aside, your natural human being will shine through as well.

Glossary for Chapter 6: Emotional Healing

1. **Emotional Wounds:** Deep psychological and emotional injuries often resulting from past traumas, negative experiences, or unresolved conflicts. These wounds can influence current behavior and emotional responses.

2. **Self-Awareness:** The conscious knowledge of one's own character, feelings, motives, and desires. It involves being mindful of one's emotions, thoughts, and behaviors.

3. **Mindfulness:** The practice of staying present and fully engaging with the current moment, observing thoughts and emotions without judgment. Mindfulness helps in recognizing and processing emotional wounds.

4. **Acceptance:** The act of recognizing and embracing reality as it is, without trying to change or resist it. In the context of emotional healing, acceptance involves acknowledging and accepting one's emotions and past experiences.

5. **Forgiveness:** The process of letting go of resentment, anger, or bitterness towards oneself or others. Forgiveness is a crucial step in emotional healing, allowing individuals to move forward without being weighed down by past hurts.

6. **Triggers:** Specific events, words, or situations that provoke strong emotional responses, often linked to past experiences or unresolved issues. Recognizing triggers is essential for managing emotional reactions.

7. **Self-Compassion:** Treating oneself with kindness and understanding, especially during difficult times. It involves being gentle with oneself in the face of failure or suffering.

8. **Healing Practices:** Activities and exercises that promote emotional healing and self-care, such as meditation,

creative expression, and physical exercise. These practices help release emotional tension and foster well-being.

9. **Therapist:** A trained professional who helps individuals process and heal from emotional wounds, providing guidance and support through therapeutic techniques.

10. **Curiosity Technique:** A method of approaching one's thoughts and reactions with curiosity, shifting from a reactive state to an investigative state. This technique helps uncover the root causes of patterns and behaviors.

11. **Pattern Interruption:** The process of breaking negative patterns of behavior and thought. It involves consciously intervening to create space for new, more positive behaviors to emerge.

12. **Emotional Resilience:** The ability to adapt to and recover from emotional challenges and stress. It involves developing coping strategies and maintaining a positive outlook.

13. **Self-Reflection:** The practice of introspection and examining one's thoughts, feelings, and behaviors. Self-reflection helps in understanding and addressing emotional wounds.

14. **Letting Go Ritual:** A symbolic activity designed to help release emotional baggage and negative feelings. Examples include writing down feelings and burning the paper or releasing it into the water.

15. **Core Beliefs:** Fundamental beliefs about oneself, others, and the world that shape thoughts, behaviors, and emotions. These beliefs often operate unconsciously and influence how we perceive and react to situations.

References for Chapter 6: Emotional Healing

Here are some relevant studies, books, and videos from sociology, psychology, and social anthropology to support the concepts discussed in Chapter Six: Emotional Healing:

Studies and Books

1. Rogers, C. R. (1961). *On Becoming a Person: A Therapist's View of Psychotherapy*. **Houghton Mifflin.** *The Evolution of Psychological Healing (ScienceDirect)*

This study explores the various methods of psychological healing, both formal and informal, such as family support, peer sharing, and professional mental health treatment. It emphasizes the importance of emotional healing as an evolutionary adaptive function, providing a broad perspective on how different healing practices have developed over time.

2. Anthropology of Emotion (Oxford Bibliographies)

This comprehensive synthesis of the anthropology of emotion reviews major works in the field and discusses the relevance of philosophical and psychological findings. It highlights how different cultures perceive and manage emotions, which is crucial for understanding diverse approaches to emotional healing.

3. Medical Sociology in Africa: Understanding Health, Illness, and Healing (Oxford University Press)

This book discusses the sociological aspects of health, illness, and healing, with a focus on African contributions to these fields. It provides insights into how different cultural contexts shape the understanding and practices of emotional healing.

4. Psychological Anthropology: Exploring the Human Mind Across Cultures (ScienceDirect)

This overview of psychological anthropology covers various perspectives within the field, including cultural psychology and ethnopsychology. It addresses topics such as personal identity, selfhood, and emotion, offering a cross-cultural perspective on emotional healing practices.

Videos

1. Healing Trauma: How to Start Feeling Better by Psych2Go

This video provides practical advice on how to begin the process of emotional healing, including recognizing emotional wounds and engaging in self care practices. It offers insights into the psychological processes involved in healing trauma.

2. The Science of Emotional Resilience by TED-Ed

This video explores the concept of emotional resilience and how individuals can develop the ability to recover from emotional setbacks. It emphasizes the role of emotional healing in building resilience.

3. Understanding and Healing Emotional Wounds by Academy of Ideas

This video delves into the mechanisms of emotional healing and provides practical steps for addressing and overcoming emotional wounds. It offers a philosophical and psychological perspective on healing.

"When you change the way you look at things, the things you look at change." -Dr. Wayne Dyer

Chapter Seven
Accepting What Is

Prelude

When I first heard Dr. Dyer quote the line in his 2004 PBS special "The Power of Intention," it prompted me to reflect deeply on my own life. I discovered that not only did the quote resonate with me, but every shift in my perspective also altered my view of the world. Each change in how I saw a single event or circumstance led to a corresponding adjustment in my reality. This repeated process shifted my perceptions of people and situations, attracting new connections while those aligned with my old perspective either changed or naturally drifted away.

On a personal note, I'm often in awe of what flows through me as I write this book. It humbles me to witness a consciousness greater than I can even imagine. I used to experience this same deep emotion when singing bhajans—spiritual songs that honor different aspects of God and the path to realization. The emotion would overwhelm me, and I'd find myself in tears as I sang. This deep connection to my experiences is something I strive to share with you throughout this book.

Introduction

Acceptance is an incredible tool for personal growth and emotional well-being. It involves recognizing and embracing reality as it is without trying to change or resist it. By accepting what is, we can find peace and clarity, allowing us to move forward with greater resilience and understanding.

The Power of Acceptance

Acceptance means acknowledging reality without judgment or resistance. It allows us to see situations clearly and respond with greater wisdom and compassion. Ultimately, acceptance is freedom.

An Example of Accepting What Is

During a session, Andie expressed her disappointment with the outcome of her Sacred Breath experience. She felt a strong need to control the process, expecting a specific outcome. Andie shared how she tried to sit up and breathe a certain way, hoping to achieve the expected results. However, this control seemed to interfere with her ability to fully engage with the experience.

I suggested to Andie that her perspective might be limiting her. She was so focused on achieving a specific outcome that she couldn't see what was actually happening. Just like in another experience where she had no control, she needed to let go of her expectations with the Sacred Breath.

Her attempts to control the outcome had prevented her from achieving her goals. She felt she was missing out compared to others, and this comparison and need for control were recurring patterns in her life. I emphasized the importance of patience with both the process and her own journey, advising her to stop comparing herself to others.

Andie admitted she was nervous about the little time left and feared she would not make a breakthrough. I reminded her that she had been expressing this fear for weeks and that changes were happening, even if they didn't meet her expectations. I explained that she might have to accept dealing with these challenges for the rest of her life, which is difficult to accept but essential for reducing their power over her.

She questioned the purpose of doing the month-long program if she would continue to face these issues. I emphasized that the point was to get it under control by not controlling and not to expect to eliminate her problem entirely. I explained that resisting the issue only gave it more power. By accepting it as a possibility in her life, she could diminish its control over her.

I also reminded her that change takes time. Just because it seemed like others were having breakthroughs did not mean hers would not come. I shared my personal experience with a core belief of worthlessness. By accepting this belief as part of myself, I reduced its impact. It affected me only when I was vulnerable, but no longer dominated my life. Acceptance isn't resignation; it's about recognizing and working with reality.

Andie struggled with this concept, feeling it contradicted her expectations of a miracle cure. I assured her that while miracles are possible, they require acceptance and alignment with reality. True acceptance means acknowledging and working with our challenges, not fighting against them.

By the end of our discussion, Andie began to understand the importance of acceptance. She realized that expecting a specific outcome led to disappointment while accepting what is allowed for a more peaceful and resilient approach to life's challenges.

Andie's one-month course was over, and she was getting on the boat to leave, but she had no remorse and understood that change happens in its own time when we have given up control and eliminated forced change.

She hugged me goodbye and said, "Thank you, Norman. I think I learned what I came here for—self-acceptance and not comparing myself to others. I'm going home a changed woman, but not in the way I expected."

We all said our farewells. Several other course participants went to the airport on the neighboring island together.

I had just gotten back to our retreat center when I received a call from Andie.

"It just happened!" she said. "I got it! With your help, I'm here. My issue just resolved itself. It was the controlling all along. That was my real issue. That is what I came to heal. When I let go of controlling my life and decided to flow with life, my problem disappeared. I feel free. I am so happy. Thank you, Norman!"

"You did the work, not me," I just said. "Look over here and consider this thing here."

Difference Between Acceptance and Resignation

Acceptance is an active process of embracing reality, while resignation is a passive state of giving up. But you haven't given up. You feel a secret anger at yourself or the situation. And you feel resentment behind that false narrative of resignation.

Acceptance empowers us to take meaningful action, whereas resignation leaves us feeling helpless and stuck.

During our session, Andie voiced her fears about never overcoming her challenges. This fear can lead to resignation, where one stops trying to improve or understand their situation. I explained that true acceptance involves recognizing the possibility of dealing with these challenges for a long time but not letting them dominate her life. By accepting rather than resisting, we reduce their power over us.

Benefits of Acceptance

1. **Reduces stress and anxiety:** Letting go of the need to control everything allows us to release tension and find peace.

2. **Enhances emotional resilience and adaptability:** Acceptance helps us to come back from setbacks and adapt to new circumstances.
3. **Promotes inner peace and clarity:** Embracing reality as it brings a sense of calm and understanding.

Practicing Acceptance

1. **Mindfulness:** Stay present and observe your thoughts and emotions without judgment. In our sessions, I often remind participants to focus on their breath and the present moment, allowing them to experience what arises without trying to change it.
2. **Self-Compassion:** Treat yourself with kindness and understanding, especially during difficult times. Andie's journey showed that accepting our flaws and struggles with compassion is essential for healing.
3. **Letting Go:** Release the need to control outcomes and embrace uncertainty. Andie's story illustrates how letting go of specific expectations can open us to new and unexpected experiences.

My Challenge With Acceptance

As you read through my story, note the key points and reflect on your own experiences. You might also consider creating 3x5 cards to focus on one point each day.

Key Point: Acceptance doesn't mean resignation—it's about embracing the present circumstances without self-blame or bitterness.

Since 2013, I have struggled with a progressing problem with my back. Initially, it showed up as a tingling in my feet after I got up from sitting for a while. I would have to walk around in circles to get rid of the tingling. I went to chiropractors, osteopaths, and massage therapists. But the problem persisted. Within a year, the pain spread to my legs, making standing and walking increasingly difficult. It became so severe that walking even 50 feet was a challenge. My doctor ordered X-rays and an MRI.

Key Point: The first step toward acceptance is acknowledging reality, even when it's not what you want to hear.

The diagnosis revealed several issues with my lower spine. On New Year's morning in 2018, I stood up and collapsed in intense pain. The doctor told me that surgery was inevitable, but even then, there was only a 50% chance of success. At that time, I was grappling with the recent end of my marriage and trying to recover from that shock. I was in Thailand, trying to start a business, and there I was, on the floor, crawling to get to my telephone. I ultimately had to abandon my business and eventually file for bankruptcy.

I had no choice but to accept that surgery was necessary. I returned to America, underwent three spinal surgeries, and was left with a cane, a slow walk, and poor balance. However, I could still walk with assistance.

Key Point: Acceptance often requires letting go of control and trusting in something greater—whether it be faith, love, or simply the process.

Throughout this period, my spiritual reserves were a saving grace. Despite living a reclusive life for over seven years, I was never lonely, often going weeks without speaking to anyone. Without these spiritual reserves, I might have succumbed to anger and bitterness. I lost my partner, faced bankruptcy, and lost mobility, yet I managed to hold onto a few clients and continue doing what I love.

Key Point: Self-reflection and solitude can help build resilience, offering you the chance to rediscover who you are beyond the pain.

Those seven years were a time of getting to know myself on a very deep level. I discovered how much I truly loved myself, life, and people.

I accepted my fate. I learned how to live with the most intense pain without serious painkillers. Even now, when I get out of bed, I spend the first few seconds hanging onto the walls until the pain subsides. Then, my day is pretty pain-free.

The doctor that I was seeing was surprised that over the time I was experiencing so much pain and life challenges that I hadn't become resentful and cruel. Pain can do that to you.

Key Point: Acceptance isn't just about physical circumstances—it's about choosing not to let your struggles define you or turn you bitter.

Had I allowed resentment or resignation to dominate my life, I wouldn't have been able to learn so much about myself. Accepting my wife's departure prevented years of bitterness. When we reunited after six years, I told her she was the love of my life.

She responded, "I don't know what to say to that."

I told her, "There is nothing to say or do. It just is."

This liberated me.

As I drove away that day, Cream's song "I Feel Free" played in my head, and I experienced a profound sense of self-love and freedom. Acceptance of what is allowed me to remove blame and avoid harboring resentment. My spine issue was genetic—nothing to be angry about with my ancestors.

Key Point: True acceptance allows for forgiveness—both of others and yourself—freeing you from the weight of bitterness.

I have traversed hardship and pain in many ways. And the result is I really love myself. We had a great time together, myself and me. LOL

Key Point: Self-love, built through hardship, becomes a foundation for resilience and peace.

Techniques for Practicing Acceptance:

Meditation:

My teacher in Bangalore once told me, "Son, who's your best friend?" I answered, "My wife, Mother." "No, son," she said. "Your mantra is your best friend. It will always be there for you throughout your life. Everything else comes and goes." She was right. While wives and friends may come and go, my mantra has remained a constant source of peace, internal space, and presence. It has provided me with the strength I needed during life's hardships.

A Personal Experience:

I once believed my meditation practice was superior, considering all other techniques secondary. After two decades of meditation, I engaged in a conversation with someone who practiced a completely different form of meditation. We discussed our experiences.

I shared it with him, and he just nodded all the way through. Then he told me one of his, and I found myself nodding all the way through.

Determined to outdo him, I recounted one of my most extraordinary meditation experiences, assuming it would impress him. Yet, he merely nodded again and shared one of his most profound experiences.

At that point, I thought, 'This guy knows his stuff.'

From that day on, my idea about forms of meditation being better or worse from one to the other changed. Not only that, the type of meditation that you need in life can change as you grow.

A Story by Ram Dass

Another example to bring this point home is a story I saw Ram Dass tell on a video.

He was speaking on stage and had decided to share some of his far-out spiritual experiences that happened through meditation. Sitting in the front row was this little old woman.

He thought to himself, this is a pretty far-out place for an old grandmother to be, in an audience with a bunch of spiritual seekers. (This was back in a time when spiritual seekers were a rarity in America.)

As he was telling his stories of wild spiritual experiences and finding profound teachers all over SE Asia and India. The little old lady would nod her head in agreement. After sharing a couple of stories and seeing that she hadn't left in dismay but was still nodding in agreement, he kept increasing the far-out stories.

Finally, Ram Dass gave up. He thought to himself, "This lady has to have some incredible technique to have had all these experiences." So, he decided to try to find her at the end of the talk to see who her guru was and what techniques she was practicing.

After looking around for her, he finally found her. He asked her what her main spiritual practice was. She responded, "Oh, sonny, I crochet."

This anecdote, combined with my own experiences, taught me a valuable lesson: there is no single "right" technique. What matters is the practice that resonates with you. Without meditation, my life would be drastically different.

I often recommend a mantra meditation, but what I mean is a meditation that puts you in a clear state of observation of yourself and your world.

Practices:

1. **Meditation**: Practice mindfulness meditation or mantra meditation or any technique that creates the ability to stay present and observe your thoughts and emotions. With mindfulness meditation focus on your breath and allow yourself to be fully present in the moment.

2. **Self-Compassion Exercises**: Engage in self-compassion exercises, such as writing to yourself from the perspective of a compassionate friend or practicing self-compassionate affirmations.

3. **Letting Go Ritual**: Develop a letting go ritual, such as writing down what you need to release and symbolically letting it go by burning the paper or releasing it into the water.

Integration of Session Content:

Andie struggled to accept her situation because she felt accepting meant giving up. I explained to her that acceptance isn't about giving up or resigning to a fate. It's about acknowledging the reality of where you are so that you can work with it instead of fighting it.

For instance, I struggled with a core belief of worthlessness. By accepting this belief as part of my current reality, rather than resisting it, I was able to diminish its control over me. Acceptance allowed me to recognize that while this belief existed, it didn't have to dominate my life. Similarly, Andie needed to see that by accepting her feelings, she could begin to loosen their hold and make space for change.

Conclusion:

Acceptance is not about surrendering or resigning to our fate. It's about recognizing and embracing our reality, allowing us to move forward with greater clarity and resilience. By practicing acceptance through mindfulness, meditation, self-compassion, and letting go, we can transform our challenges into opportunities for growth.

Glossary for Chapter 7: Accepting What Is

1. **Acceptance**: The act of recognizing and embracing reality as it is, without trying to change or resist it.

2. **Self-Awareness**: Conscious knowledge of one's own character, feelings, motives, and desires.

3. **Mindfulness**: The practice of being present and fully engaged with the current moment, observing thoughts and emotions without judgment.

4. **Self-Compassion**: Treating oneself with kindness and understanding, especially during difficult times.

5. **Letting Go**: The process of releasing the need to control outcomes and embracing uncertainty.

6. **Resignation**: A passive state of giving up, often accompanied by feelings of helplessness and resentment.

7. **Inner Peace**: A state of mental and emotional calmness and clarity.

8. **Emotional Resilience**: The ability to adapt to and recover from emotional challenges and stress.

9. **Adaptability**: The capacity to adjust to new conditions and circumstances.

10. **Emotional Triggers**: Specific stimuli that provoke strong emotional reactions due to unresolved past experiences.

11. **Personal Growth**: The process of improving oneself through self-awareness, acceptance, and embracing challenges.

12. **Meditation**: A practice that involves focusing the mind on a particular object, thought, or activity to achieve a mentally clear and emotionally calm state.

13. **Mantra**: A word or sound repeated to aid concentration in meditation.

14. **Ritual**: A set of actions performed for their symbolic value, often used in the context of letting go or embracing new beginnings.

15. **Core Belief**: Fundamental beliefs about oneself that influence thoughts, behaviors, and emotions.

16. **Self-Reflection**: The practice of introspection and examining one's thoughts, feelings, and behaviors to gain insight and understanding.

17. **Emotional Healing**: The process of acknowledging and addressing emotional wounds, allowing for recovery and personal growth.

18.

References for Chapter 7: Accepting What Is

Here are some relevant studies, books, and videos from sociology, psychology, and social anthropology to support the concepts discussed in Chapter 7: Accepting What Is:

Studies and Books

1. **Psychological Anthropology: Exploring the Human Mind Across Cultures**

This overview provides a comprehensive look at how cognition, emotion, and motivation are shaped in different sociocultural settings. It discusses the importance of acceptance and understanding in dealing with various life situations, highlighting the interplay between individual psychology and cultural factors (ScienceDirect).

2. **Anthropology vs. Sociology: Understanding Human Behavior**

This resource explains the differences between anthropology and sociology, focusing on how these disciplines study human behavior. Anthropology looks at individual and cultural specifics, while sociology examines group behaviors and social structures. Understanding these perspectives can help in grasping how acceptance varies across cultures and social contexts (ThoughtCo).

3. **Social Psychology, Anthropology, and the Behavioral Sciences**

This study explores the integration of social psychology, anthropology, and other behavioral sciences. It emphasizes the importance of acceptance in psychological well-being and the role of social structures in shaping individual behaviors and attitudes (JSTOR).

Videos

1.The Power of Acceptance by TEDx Talks

This video discusses the concept of acceptance and its significance in personal growth and emotional well-being. It includes practical advice on how to cultivate acceptance in daily life.

2.Practicing Acceptance: A Guide to Letting Go by Psych2Go

This video provides an overview of acceptance, differentiating it from resignation. It offers practical tips and exercises for embracing acceptance and letting go of control, aligning with the themes discussed in your chapter.

3.Understanding and Embracing Acceptance by Academy of Ideas

This video delves into the psychological and philosophical aspects of acceptance, offering insights into how acceptance can lead to a more fulfilling and peaceful life.

A Sadhu realizes that sharing a cave with another Sadhu makes the path to oneness with God a bit *too* crowded. So he kicks the other Sadhu out.

Chapter Eight
Relationship Dynamics

Introduction

During my quest for enlightenment, I encountered two main spiritual paths: the path of the "Recluse" and the path of the "Householder." This was the first main separation of spiritual aspirants. The path of the recluse seemed to be revered and claimed to be the most difficult of the two paths. It just didn't make sense to me based on my own experiences. All the recluse has to do is deal with his mind and the austerity of his cave. Whereas a householder is constantly dealing with their ego and another human being, and if they have children, what that brings to the dynamics. How can you be one with God if you can't get along with another human being?

For me, relationships themselves are a form of spiritual practice, a preparation for union. Many spiritual teachers talk about surrendering your ego or the death of the ego in order to realize God or to become Enlightened. Relationship with a partner is surrendering to the relationship. Not surrendering to the other person.

A simple example: I would like to buy myself a new motorcycle. We want a cabin in the mountains to get away from everyday life. The "We" statement must always prevail. [And, of course, there are a few exceptions to this rule. What I mean by this is that sometimes, the partner cannot be a part of a decision-making process.]

Whatever gets in the way of becoming a "We" is your spiritual growth. Your partner becomes your teacher, and you become your partner's teacher. Believe me, whatever you haven't dealt with in your life will come up in your relationship. If you ever want to know how you are doing to become enlightened or one with God, have a look at your relationships.

As Katherine Woodward Thomas aptly puts it, "Human beings are relational beings." This insight came from a discussion about the New Age notion that we should not need others. Although recluses demonstrate that one can survive alone, it contradicts our inherent nature.

I spent seven years reclusive and without much human contact. But, during that time I was engaged in an active search for, "Who is Norman Brown." I found that, yes, I can do it. But, I really realized how important human interaction is to our wellbeing. Once I got to know myself, I then wanted to return to interacting with others from this new perspective.

We thrive and grow from our relationships, which are fundamental to our lives, shaping our experiences, growth, and emotional well-being. Understanding the dynamics of relationships can help us navigate them with greater awareness and intention, fostering healthier and more fulfilling connections with others. Contrary to some beliefs, we need each other to grow and be our best. There will always be needs that you can't meet on your own. Having our needs met fulfills us and gives us space to see the world from a healthier perspective. From there, all possibilities can arise.

The Foundation of Relationship Dynamics

Relationships are built on a complex interplay of emotions, behaviors, and expectations. Each person brings their unique history, beliefs, and emotional baggage into the relationship, influencing how they interact with their partner. In other words, you come into a relationship from your reality. If you understand that, you will combine two realities into one space, creating an interplay of change and growth. If one of the two thinks they are the only one living in the actual reality, you will have problems.

Case Study: John and Lisa

In one of my courses, John and Lisa, a couple in their 30s, approached me at the end of a year-long sabbatical. Both had high-level jobs and had decided to take time off to explore their life together. By the time they reached my retreat center, Lisa was seven months pregnant, an unexpected development, and they anticipated a divorce upon returning home.

They struggled with communication and emotional connection. John felt Lisa was distant, while Lisa found John's need for constant reassurance overwhelming. Through the course, they discovered that John's need for reassurance stemmed from a childhood fear of abandonment, and Lisa's distancing was a defense mechanism from previous suffocating relationships.

By understanding these underlying issues, John and Lisa began communicating more openly about their fears and needs. John practiced giving Lisa space without taking it personally, while Lisa made an effort to reassure John without feeling overwhelmed. Over time, they developed a healthier dynamic where both felt understood and respected. They returned home and decided together that John would be the moneymaker and Lisa would raise their child and care for their home life. The result: no divorce and a workable plan for the future.

Understanding Relationship Dynamics

Relationship dynamics refer to the patterns of interaction and behavior between individuals in a relationship. Various factors shape these dynamics, including communication styles, emotional needs, past experiences, and individual personalities.

Types of Relationship Dynamics

Healthy Dynamics: Involve mutual respect, trust, effective communication, and emotional support. If any of these are damaged, you are on a path to the end of the relationship.

Unhealthy Dynamics: Characterized by patterns of control, manipulation, lack of communication, emotional dependency, maintaining the status quo, and withholding needs. If you feel any of these are happening, you might want to try some helpful techniques to overcome them.

Identifying Unhealthy Dynamics

Pay attention to recurring patterns of conflict, misunderstanding, and emotional distress in your relationships. Recognize signs of unhealthy dynamics, such as constant criticism, lack of trust, emotional manipulation, and withholding of needs.

Building Healthy Relationship Dynamics

Effective Communication: Practice active listening, express your thoughts and feelings clearly, and validate the emotions of others.

Emotional Awareness: Be aware of your own emotional needs and those of others and strive to create a balance between them. The best relationships are when both parties meet the needs of the other naturally, without asking for them. It is always a good thing to sit with your partner and identify each other's needs and what you have to contribute to their needs.

Boundaries: Set and respect boundaries to maintain a sense of individuality and mutual respect in the relationship. After reading the chapter on boundaries in this book, sit together and discuss this.

Conflict Resolution: Address conflicts openly and constructively, focusing on finding solutions rather than assigning blame. If you are upset, discussing a conflict is not the time.

Take a walk, watch TV, or read a book. You will quickly move through anger or resentment and be able to come back and meet for a constructive discussion.

Sometimes, you want to feel justified in your hurt and anger. Give yourself a set amount of time for self-pity.

I usually tell myself, "Okay, you've got 30 minutes of self-pity. Go for it. Go as deep into it as you want. But when that thirty minutes is up, it's done." Remember, emotions are experienced as eternal or unending. When you are at the peak, you have no room for self-examination or the ability to examine a situation clearly with a partner or anyone else, for that matter.

Critical Concepts in Relationship Dynamics

Communication: Effective communication is crucial for healthy relationships. It involves expressing your thoughts and feelings and actively listening to your partner.

Misunderstandings often arise from assumptions and unspoken expectations (your reality). Clarifying these can prevent conflicts and strengthen the bond. Remember, a relationship has two realities, each with its own dynamics that are unknown to the other.

Emotional Baggage: Everyone carries emotional baggage from past experiences. Recognizing and addressing this baggage is essential for a healthy relationship. Unresolved issues can manifest as triggers, leading to conflicts. Being aware of these

144

triggers can help in managing them constructively. You think a relationship is about love and building a life together, and yes, it is that. But it is also an unconscious agreement to show each other where you need to grow. If you can look at it that way, it is much less complicated to accept when your partner does something that causes you to step off the deep end and realize that you are not the incredibly spiritual person you thought you were. Or that they are not always that excellent source of milk and honey that flows inside you when you are in their presence.

Boundaries: Healthy boundaries are vital for maintaining individuality and respect in a relationship. They help protect your emotional and physical space. Communicating your boundaries clearly and respecting your partner's boundaries fosters mutual respect and trust. Chapter five on boundaries should help you both get there after you become familiar with your own and work on having healthy boundaries in life.

Trust and Vulnerability: Trust is the foundation of any relationship. It is built over time through consistent actions and honesty. Being vulnerable with your partner strengthens the emotional connection and allows for deeper intimacy. The idea of falling entirely into the complete trust of your partner right away is asking for trouble. Give it time and let it build. It isn't fun to find out that you put all your trust in someone who is not trustworthy. If you are someone who does that and this is the person that you attract, then that says a lot about what you believe about yourself. And they have served you in the relationship. Their job was to wake you up to that belief to see that it doesn't serve you.

Conflict Resolution: Conflicts are inevitable in any relationship. How they are handled determines the health of the relationship. Approaching conflicts with a resolution mindset rather than blame can lead to growth and understanding. And, of course, before trying to resolve it, wait to get back to ground zero so you can have a healthy discussion.

Meeting Each Other's Needs: This is not discussed enough. It was too late when I finally realized my needs in a relationship. After already being in a relationship with my last wife for some time, I asked her to sit down with me and discuss what we both need in a relationship to see if this area was compatible. So, we sat down with our two lists, and it was incredible to find out that we were incompatible in this area of the relationship.

For example, I needed a partner that would be a partner in life, business, and otherwise. I had learned in a previous relationship how wonderful this was and how much it nourished me. She wanted a relationship where we had separate lives. Where each one is doing their own thing in life. Then we would come together to share a space. She tried to meet my needs, and I tried to meet hers. She wanted to support me in what I was doing, and I tried to give her space to do whatever she wanted. It just didn't work. No matter how much we loved each other. It just fostered resentment of the other. Eventually, this was one of the major downfalls of the marriage. It took ten years for our lacks to bring down the marriage. But, in the end, it was one of the major nails in the coffin that was our relationship.

Techniques for Building Healthy Relationships

1. **Active Listening:** Practice active listening by giving your full attention to your partner, acknowledging their feelings, and responding thoughtfully. Reflective listening can be particularly effective when you repeat what your partner has said to ensure understanding.

2. **Listening with the Heart:** This is the practice of being present while someone is talking. It comes with mindfulness techniques and developing self-awareness

through meditation. This technique can be applied after you have mastered active listening. With this technique, there is only speaking and listening happening. There is no one analyzing. There is only an intention happening— an intention of a presence of love and a purpose of hearing. There is no definition of self and no definition of other. Meaning only awareness is there in both. When this indeed happens, the mind shuts up, and a space is created for whatever will happen to happen.

3. **Expressing Emotions Constructively:** Use "I" statements to share your feelings without placing blame. For example, say "I feel hurt when…" rather than "You always…". This fosters honest communication and a safe space for both partners. You might start with, "This is just how I feel right now. My emotions make me believe this, but I want to work through it with your help to gain clarity." Avoid suggesting they do the same, as they may not be ready, which could trigger them. Approaching the conversation seeking help, rather than "fixing" things, prevents the other person from feeling blamed or inadequate. Each person is responsible for their own emotions. If they're not willing to engage, that's their choice—and it will reveal whether this is a relationship that can last.

4. **Setting and Respecting Boundaries:** Discuss and establish boundaries in your relationship. Ensure that both partners are comfortable with and respect these boundaries. Regularly revisit and adjust boundaries as needed to accommodate changes in the relationship. Again, doing the chapter on boundaries will help with this.

5. **Building Trust:** Consistency and reliability are crucial to building trust. Follow through on promises and be honest

with your partner. Honesty creates an easy flow in life. Being fearful of a relationship's loss and not being honest is a perfect way to destroy a relationship. Address any breaches of trust openly and work towards rebuilding it together.

6. **Practicing Vulnerability:** Share your fears, hopes, and dreams with your partner. Being vulnerable fosters deeper intimacy. Support your partner in their vulnerability by being empathetic and non-judgmental.

Personal Example of Listening with the Heart

During a visit to a newfound friend in California, I felt a deep sense of camaraderie despite knowing little about him. We had met at an ashram in India, shared insightful conversations, and explored sacred sites together. He invited me to his home in California before I returned to Thailand.

One night, we were sitting on the couch talking, and he told me that his wife had died of cancer not that long ago. He had cared for her up until her passing. He was a great chef and had been cooking her meals for her. He loved her deeply and prepared the healthiest meals with the most significant amount of love he could put into each meal. He cared for her every need, bathed her, and carried her to sit near a window and outside, giving her everything she needed to be as comfortable as possible.

On her last day, she asked for her favorite meal—a dish that required ingredients he didn't have at home and would take most of the day to prepare. He was determined to honor her wish, despite knowing she wouldn't be able to keep it down. He spent hours in the kitchen, arranging for someone to stay with her while he went shopping, and even paid someone to do so when no one was available.

After a long day, he served the meal on their finest china. She managed a few bites before stopping. Shortly after, she began vomiting, and he had to clean her and change the bed sheets.

I felt a strong urge to listen with my heart. As he settled her back in bed, she passed away. Without thinking, I asked, "Tell me about this meal. What was it? How did you prepare it?" As he detailed the preparation, he suddenly confessed, "I killed my wife." He continued describing the meal without skipping a beat.

When he finished, I asked him, "How did you kill your wife?"

Overcome with sobs, he eventually managed to explain, "While preparing that meal, I was consumed by anger. I was exhausted from the past five days of little sleep and from the year dedicated to caring for her. I felt she didn't appreciate the sacrifices I made. My anger and exhaustion seeped into the meal, and I feared that negative energy contributed to her death."

Surprised, I replied, "Actually, you didn't transfer any negative energy into the meal. Your love for her was evident even then." He broke down again, and I added, "Perhaps she was trying to give you a break. She knew how much you loved this dish, and didn't you win an award for it?"

"How do you know that?" he asked, astonished.

"I'm not sure," I said. By listening with the heart, something opened up in that space, and he was able to release an emotion that had been dominating and plaguing him since her death. Imagine the pain that he was feeling. Now, it was released. He was free from it. Something that goes beyond simple explanations happens when you can listen like this. You create a space where healing can take place.

Having become accustomed to my work, I understood that my visit had a purpose beyond strengthening our friendship. Being open to life's experiences invites the possibility of miracles.

Navigating Cultural Differences in Our Relationship

My girlfriend is Thai, and I'm from the U.S., so we face a big language barrier and significant cultural differences. One of the more recent challenges we encountered was this:

We had agreed to build bungalows where people could visit, and I could hold courses. We looked at various bungalow building techniques and layouts of other homestay resorts here in Northern Thailand. She decided to dedicate a third of her rice field land to the project. Initially, we had talked about using another piece of land she owned next to the rice field. However, after looking into it, she realized it would take two more years before we could even access that land.

When she shared this dilemma with me, I suggested discussing it with the renter to see if we could start construction sooner. However, the renter immediately rejected this idea, insisting that we couldn't proceed until the lease ended. A week later, I was shocked to see photos of a backhoe digging a pond and preparing a portion of her rice field for construction. In a Western relationship, we would likely have had a thorough discussion before taking such a step. While the ultimate decision would be hers since it was her land, there would have been more back-and-forth conversation.

On the day the backhoe arrived and started digging, I had no idea this was happening. I wasn't even there. She sent me a series of photos of a place she admired, asking if I liked it. I said yes. A couple of hours later, she sent more photos of the backhoe at work. I had no clue this was the plan. In the past, this would have upset me, leading to an argument.

I tried to talk to her about doing this without us fully discussing it. She explained that we couldn't use the land we had originally wanted and pointed out that she had shown me the pond style she liked. It was clear to her: to move forward without waiting two years, she had to use part of her rice field. And I had agreed to the pond idea because she'd shown me what she envisioned.

In her mind, it was simple. It's her land, and we'd already agreed to build this place. From there, it was up to her to make it happen. We'd already agreed on who would pay for what.

Recognizing this as a cultural difference helped me accept the situation. She made a significant sacrifice, dedicating a third of her rice field's income to create a space for us to host guests. In her view, this was her contribution as a loving partner. Had I clung to my Western approach to decision-making, I might have caused unnecessary conflict and hurt her deeply.

Conclusion

Understanding and improving relationship dynamics is a continuous process that requires effort and commitment from both partners. We can foster healthier and more fulfilling relationships by focusing on effective communication, recognizing emotional baggage, setting healthy boundaries, building trust, and practicing vulnerability.

Relationships are a journey of growth and discovery. Embrace this journey with an open heart and a willingness to learn, and you will find that the rewards are well worth the effort. As you navigate your relationships with greater awareness and intention, you will create connections that support your well-being and personal growth, enriching your life in profound and meaningful ways.

Personal note: In 2015 and 2016, I read both of Katherine Woodward Thomas' books, *Calling in the One* and *Conscious Uncoupling*. I also took her classes for coaching these two books. These books, both New York Times best-sellers, provided powerful insights and were instrumental as I recovered from my previous relationship. Her guidance remains a valuable resource for me.

Glossary for Chapter 8: Relationship Dynamics

1. **Relationship Dynamics:** The patterns of interaction and behavior between individuals in a relationship, shaped by communication styles, emotional needs, past experiences, and individual personalities.

2. **Healthy Dynamics:** Relationship patterns that involve mutual respect, trust, effective communication, and emotional support.

3. **Unhealthy Dynamics:** Patterns characterized by control, manipulation, lack of communication, emotional dependency, and withholding of needs.

4. **Effective Communication:** The practice of expressing thoughts and feelings clearly and listening actively to understand the other person's perspective.

5. **Emotional Awareness:** Being conscious of your own emotional needs and those of others, striving to create a balance between them.

6. **Boundaries:** Limits set to maintain a sense of individuality and mutual respect in relationships, protecting emotional and physical space.

7. **Conflict Resolution:** The process of addressing conflicts openly and constructively, focusing on finding solutions rather than assigning blame.

8. **Active Listening:** Fully concentrating on what is being said rather than passively hearing the message of the speaker. This involves making eye contact, not interrupting, and providing feedback.

9. **Reflective Listening:** Repeating what the other person has said to ensure understanding and to show that their perspective is valued.

10. **Expressing Emotions Constructively:** Sharing feelings honestly and openly using "I" statements to express emotions without blaming others.

11. **Triggers:** Emotional responses or reactions that are set off by specific events, words, or situations, often linked to past experiences.

12. **Building Trust:** The process of developing confidence in a partner's reliability and integrity through consistent actions and honesty.

13. **Vulnerability:** Allowing oneself to be open and honest about fears, hopes, and dreams, fostering deeper emotional intimacy.

References for Chapter 8: Relationship Dynamics

Here are some relevant studies, books, and videos from sociology, psychology, and social anthropology to support the concepts discussed in Chapter 8: Relationship Dynamics:

Studies and Books:

1. **Interpersonal Emotion Dynamics in Close Relationships (Cambridge University Press):** This book provides a comprehensive overview of how emotions play a powerful role in close relationships. It addresses how interpersonal emotion dynamics manifest and contribute to the maintenance or dissolution of relationships. This resource is valuable for understanding the emotional underpinnings of relationship dynamics.

2. **Relationships in Sociology (Oxford Bibliographies):** This resource covers a multidisciplinary approach to studying relationships, integrating perspectives from sociology, social psychology, and clinical psychology. It provides insights into how different factors such as communication styles, emotional needs, and past experiences shape relationship dynamics.

3. **Group Dynamics and Behavior (Open Textbook Library):** This text discusses the effects of group size on group dynamics, providing a foundational understanding of how relationships within small groups (dyads and triads) can be intense yet unstable. It also covers leadership styles and their impact on group cohesion and decision-making.

Videos:

1. **The Science of Relationships by TEDx Talks:** This video explores the scientific basis of relationship

dynamics, including communication, emotional intelligence, and conflict resolution. It provides practical advice for building healthier relationships.

2. **Understanding Relationship Dynamics by Psych2Go:** This video breaks down the fundamental aspects of relationship dynamics, such as the importance of boundaries, emotional awareness, and effective communication. It offers easy-to-understand explanations and actionable tips for improving relationship health.

3. **Emotional Dynamics in Relationships by Academy of Ideas:** This video delves into the emotional aspects of relationships, discussing how emotions influence interactions and relationship stability. It highlights the importance of emotional awareness and regulation in maintaining healthy dynamics.

What You Put Your Attention On In Life Grows In Your Life—Maharishi Mahesh Yogi

Chapter Nine
Bonus Chapter

Introduction

In this chapter, I build on ideas from previous sections, drawing on materials such as books and videos that have profoundly inspired me. Now that you've spent some time with me, I'll delve deeper into my personal sources of inspiration and experiences on this journey. I tend to have intense emotional reactions to both fictional narratives and real-life events, whether they involve myself or others.

This sensitivity has heightened as I've progressed along my path, making me selective about the media I consume. I want to emphasize that what I share here is based on my experiences and may not apply to everyone. The outcome is that I can sometimes be right there with the person I am working with and know their experiences.

How I Became Aware of My Empathic Ability

The first time I became aware of this was when I was standing in front of an elevator at a community college in Phoenix, Arizona. As I stood there, the elevator bell dinged, and the doors opened. A rather large African American woman stood right there in front of me. Our eyes met as the doors opened, and something extraordinary happened to me.

I was suddenly her. I knew everything about her and how she was experiencing life. I knew things about her family and what she was doing there at the school. We were both kind of frozen at that moment, and everything was experienced in slow motion. She had a really strange look on her face, and I felt that we were both very embarrassed. People moved around both of us and continued on their way. She managed a smile and stepped out of the elevator. I walked past her into the elevator, kind of dumbfounded. She turned, looked back as if to say something, and went on about her business.

As the elevator ascended, I was overwhelmed with a sense of being two people simultaneously. I felt an intense compassion for this woman and her life, coupled with a growing fear that I was losing my sanity. I struggled to make sense of what had happened, feeling emotionally and physically drained. By the time the elevator reached my floor, I was exhausted. I sank into a nearby couch, hoping to find solace. This was not the first strange experience I had encountered since beginning meditation, so I reassured myself that it would pass. After about twenty minutes, the sensation of being that other person gradually faded.

At the time, I just chalked it up to one of those experiences that can happen when you have been meditating for some time. I continued to have similar experiences, but not as strong as that one. A couple of years later, I shared this experience with someone who understood what I had gone through. She identified me as an Empath and explained that while I lacked control over this ability, there were ways to manage it. She introduced me to a protective mantra that has since become a valuable tool. This mantra helps me maintain control and provides a sense of safety, whether I'm traveling by car, plane, or any other means. I don't rely on it excessively; rather, I've integrated it into my life as a practical measure.

I will share it with you. If you are empathic, then you know how much extraneous noise there is in any environment. My thought noise level decreased almost immediately.

Another Empathic Experience

On a drive from Iowa to Kansas City for my monthly Air Force Reserves weekend, I realized I had forgotten to use my new mantra. The four-lane highway stretched out ahead, empty and serene. I was alone, enjoying the quiet moments of solitude. As I tried to refocus my wandering mind on the present, I began to feel an unexpected irritation.

At first, I wondered if my irritation stemmed from my mind's resistance to staying present. This thought only seemed to heighten my frustration, and soon, I was genuinely angry. I couldn't pinpoint the source of my anger, which left me feeling confused. Just then, a car sped past in the passing lane. I glanced over and saw two people arguing intensely. At that moment, my anger reached its peak, but as the car moved out of sight, my irritation gradually faded. It dawned on me that the anger I had been feeling was connected to their emotional turmoil.

Over time, this realization became a routine practice, and I used it frequently. What I learned most was how easily I could connect with others on a profound level. Although it took years before I fully harnessed my empathic abilities, this technique proved invaluable. The key takeaway is that reducing mental noise greatly enhances self-awareness.

The Mantra for Personal Protection

I will go through it line by line, and after each line, I will give you some instructions that will help you experience the full power of this mantra. Sit with your eyes closed and repeat each line of the mantra. You will have to repeat it with your eyes open until you have it memorized. After that, you repeat it with your eyes closed using these instructions. I use the word "Envision," and you can use "Imagine" or "Think of"–whatever works best for you.

- **I Am the Light** (Envision yourself behind a wall of white light)

- **The Light is Within Me** (Envision the wall of light moving from in front of you to within you)

- **The Light Moves Throughout Me** (Now, envision that light moving throughout your entire body. Constantly moving almost like milk)

- **The Light Surrounds Me** (Envision that the light comes out of the floor or earth and surrounds you like a white tube coming from below, encircling you and extending all the way over your head and into the universe)

- **The Light Protects Me** (Now envision that the light surrounding you has spires sticking out everywhere so that nothing can come through without being impaled on multiple spires)

- **I Am the Light** (Take ownership of the light)

- **I Am the Light** (Say it stronger)

- **I AM THE LIGHT** (Take complete ownership of the light)

Remain with closed eyes for a moment or two and notice if you feel anything. You don't have to say it over and over again. One time will suffice. On an airplane, I say this as we are taxiing before takeoff, and in the car or on a motorcycle, I say it before I go anywhere.

Of course, you can say it whenever you want. However, it works best for you. I also use it before meetings or before I enter a crowded area.

The Inner Light

One of my early experiences was both peculiar and profoundly natural. During a meditation retreat, I woke up one night to find the room bathed in a soft, pervasive light, much like a night light. The source of this light eluded me; I remembered the room being pitch black when I had turned off the lights before bed. Initially, I was a bit unsettled, wondering if someone had come into the room and accidentally left a light on when they left.

But it seemed everywhere I looked, there was this soft light. It had to have a source. So I even got out of bed and looked all around. Not seeing a source, I went back to bed.

I thought, "Oh well, it won't keep me awake." So I lay down to go to sleep. I closed my eyes. I suddenly realized that I must not be closing my eyes because I could still see the room. So, I reached up and put my hand over my face covering my eyes. But I could still see the room.

I sat up in the bed in surprise. I closed my eyes and opened them several times. I could still see everything in the room. I closed my eyes and put my hand over my eyes. I could still see the room.

Then, I started to notice that what I could see was expanding. My peripheral vision was expanding. Soon, in a few seconds, I was seeing behind me, above me, front, back, up, and down. I even did a few calculations of the location of things I saw, and when I turned the front of my face in whatever direction, that was precisely what I saw. It was there like the painting on the wall behind me and the broken baseboard to the right back behind me.

It confused me a little, and then I grabbed the pillow and put my face into it, and nothing changed in my sight. I saw the pillow on my face and the room. I thought, "This is weird. I think I'll go back to sleep."

As I lay back down, I noticed my field of vision expanding. I could see in all directions simultaneously—behind me, above me, and even through the walls into the adjoining bathroom. This was disorienting. I thought, "This is strange. I'll just lie here and perhaps eventually fall asleep."

Eventually, I realized that the light source was within me. I understood that this inner light is a reflection of who we are. It's seen by others and shapes our reality, attracting experiences that align with our subconscious beliefs. As we evolve, this inner light grows brighter, drawing more growth and love into our lives. This shift brings more peace and reduces negative thoughts.

Greater peace fosters greater awareness. The subconscious mind constantly presents our reality, offering us choices. It serves us by asking, "This is the reality you've created. Is it enough or do we continue to evolve?"

The Books, Videos, and Audios that Helped Me Along the Way

Books (They are not in chronological order)

- *Loving What Is* by Byron Katie
- *Getting the Love You Want* by Harville Hendrix, PhD
- *The Power of Now* by Eckhart Tolle
- *The Dark Side of the Light Chasers* by Debbie Ford
- *Perfect Health* by Deepak Chopra
- *Healing Trauma* by Peter Levine
- *Waking the Tiger* by Peter Levine
- *The Power of Intention* by Dr. Wayne Dyer
- *Ammachi: A Biography of Mata Amritanandamayi*
- *Daughter of Fire* by Irina Tweedie

- *I Am Harmony: A Book about Babaji* by Radhe Shyam
- *The Clan of the Cave Bear* (and the following 3 books of this series) by Jean M. Auel
- *The Education of Little Tree* by Forrest Carter
- *Siddhartha* by Hermann Hesse (I re-visit this every few years)
- *Autobiography of a Yogi* by Paramahansa Yogananda (My first spiritual book)
- *I Am That* by Nisargadatta Maharaj (Read this and forget about it)
- *Molecules of Emotion* by Dr. Candace Pert

Audio

Here I will list a few of the authors because I have listened to a lot of their audio:

- Dr. Wayne Dyer
- Ram Dass
- Byron Katie
- Bruce Lipton
- Eckhart Tolle
- Deepak Chopra
- Rupert Sheldrake
- Gangaji
- John Lennon— Imagine
- Moody Blues

Video

- Dr. Wayne Dyer
- Eckhart Tolle
- Ram Dass
- Bruce Lipton

- PBS
  - Human Instinct (4 Part Series)
  - Evolution
- What the Bleep Do We Know
- Study the movie "Matrix"

In Conclusion of This Book

When I built the retreat center on the island of Koh Phangan, Thailand, it wasn't easy to get to us. Not only did you have to find us on the internet, but you had to go all the way to Thailand to the island we were on, climb a very steep hill, and sleep in a bungalow which was only cooled with a fan in the Thai heat. You had to really want what we offered. So, by the time our guests arrived in our kitchen building, they were totally exhausted and ready to make a change.

Your life's journey is in your hands, and it's a unique path of self-discovery and personal development. There's no shame in pausing along the way. As humans, we're resilient and can endure discomfort. It's all part of our nature, our growth process.

But if you finish this book and still want more, don't worry. I have more coming. As soon as I publish this book, I will be deep into getting book two into your hands.

As we conclude, let's revisit the profound experiences.

I've come to understand that these experiences are not the ultimate goal. They're like passing clouds in the sky, here one moment and gone the next. I've learned not to cling to them or push them away. Paraphrasing, Maharishi Mahesh Yogi wisely said, "Why settle for a diamond or gold mine when you can conquer the castle at the mountain's peak, and then the entire mountain is your kingdom?"

It is my heartfelt desire that this book has inspired you, helped you gain a little more peace, and lit the spiritual fire in you.

Our Last Story

I'd like to leave you with one final story, rich in lessons. See if you can uncover them on your own.

A monk who lived in the jungles of India had made his hut near a river. One day, during meditation, he heard another monk just on the other side of the river. The monk on the other side of the river was chanting a most sacred chant and doing it all wrong.

The monk in meditation was distressed by this chanting because he was proficient in all the holy texts, and this was definitely wrong. Knowing the intricacies of this particular chant, he could not help but be distracted in his meditation.

Finally, after several days of failed meditations, he decided enough was enough. About an hour before the other monk would chant the next day, he took his little canoe and paddled across the river.

The monk on the other side of the river welcomed him with open arms and immediately offered to serve him tea. Soon they were deeply delving into all things spiritual. The monk that came to visit was pleasantly surprised to know that this monk was profoundly knowledgeable.

After a while, he had to bring up the improper chanting. He said, "Brother, I must confess. I am disturbed by how wrongly you are chanting this profound chant. Maybe I can be of assistance and teach you the proper way to chant it. Then you will receive the benefits. It is said that if chanted correctly and enough times, one will attain the Siddhi of walking on water."

His newfound brother was happy to receive any help he might have to offer. After chanting it together several times and making the necessary corrections in his chanting, the monk was happy with himself for saving his poor brother from mispronunciation.

The monk happily got into his canoe and paddled back across the river. "Tonight, my meditation will not be disturbed," he thought. Once he arrived at his hut, he hurried to prepare for his evening rituals. Soon, the other monk across the river had begun chanting.

That evening, as he prepared for his rituals, he was pleased to hear the chant performed correctly. However, his satisfaction was short-lived. The other monk soon faltered, repeatedly slipping back into the old mispronunciations.

Then, something extraordinary happened. As the monk struggled with the chant, he suddenly walked across the surface of the river, not in the water but on it. Arriving at the hut, he said, "Brother, I seem to have forgotten what you taught me. Could you show me again?"

And finally, I leave you with this.

There's a saying from an old Anheuser-Busch commercial that I saw: "You only go around once in life. Live it with all the gusto you can."

This is your journey. No one can live your life for you. When you have to jump into the box at the end of your life, and there are no regrets. Then, you have lived it with all the gusto you can!

Join the Community

- If you would like to join a group study for this book, share your answers, or seek further guidance, please contact Norman at nb879@yahoo.com or samhitaretreatcenter@gmail.com or through samhitaretreatcenter.com.

- Norman holds ongoing meditation courses and self-healing programs. Consider participating for additional support and growth.

www.ingramcontent.com/pod-product-compliance
Lightning Source LLC
Chambersburg PA
CBHW060426130626
46555CB00005B/2229